S0-BIN-560

A CALL TO THE LAITY

A CAL

Addresses on the Lay Apostola

Compiled by Reverend G E O R G E L . K A

TO THE LAITY

the Most Reverend

ICHARD J. CUSHING, D.D.

chbishop of Boston

E NEWMAN PRESS • WESTMINSTER • MARYLAND
57

Nihil obstat: Eduardus A. Cerny, S.S. D.D.
Censor Librorum
Imprimatur: ✠ Franciscus P. Keough, D.D.
Archiepiscopus Baltimorensis
die 23 Octobris, 1956

Library of Congress Catalog Card Number: 56-11413
Printed in the United States of America

Foreword

Though too many of the laity still feel that their obligations to the Church are satisfied by attending Mass, receiving the sacraments, and contributing to the Sunday collection, an ever-increasing number of splendid lay Catholics are acquiring a consciousness of their responsibility to the Church in terms of helping to meet her needs and solve her problems. Recent popes have again and again called for a zealous and apostolic laity to assist in the task of restoring all things in Christ. Indeed, the critical shortage of priests and religious facing the Church in almost every part of the world at the present time underlines the duty of lay Catholics to accept a greater share of the work of the Church. If the work is to be done, more and more of the laity must come to the assistance of the limited number of priests and religious. Such is the appeal of the present Holy Father, and such is the will of God.

Faithfully echoing the call of the supreme pontiffs, Archbishop Cushing of Boston has delivered a large number of stirring addresses to various lay groups, reminding them of their obligations and responsibilities as functioning members of the Mystical Body of Christ. Invariably these addresses are vigorous and forceful in style, original in approach, and challenging in content. In order that they may reach a much wider audience, His Excellency has graciously consented to their publication in book form.

The compiler wishes to express his gratitude to Archbishop Cushing for his cooperation and to the editors of the following publications for permission to reprint material: *The Pilot* (Boston), *The American Ecclesiastical Review* (Washington, D. C.), *The Voice of St. Jude* (Chicago), and *Marist Missions* (Framingham Centre, Mass.). To Miss Anna E. Moran of Dorchester, Mass., he is indebted for providing the copy of the address, "The Age of the Laity."

George L. Kane

January 13, 1956

Contents

One

THE LAITY IN THE CHURCH

The Apostolate of the Laity †

The apostolate of the laity—the participation of the laity in the work of the Church, under direction of their duly appointed pastors—is the twentieth century phrase to describe the proper life of the Church, the flowering in action of the faith and love of all members of the Mystical Body on earth, action that began with the first sermon preached by St. Peter after the ascension of Our Lord and continued through the ages by priest and layman side by side.

St. Paul gives us the theology of it: "For just as in one body we have many members, yet all members have not the same function, so we, the many, are one body in Christ, but severally members one of another. But we have gifts differing according to the grace that has been given us, such as prophecy to be used according to the proportion of faith; or ministry, in ministering; or he who teaches, in teaching; he who exhorts, in exhorting; he who gives, in simplicity; he who presides, with carefulness; he who shows mercy, with cheerfulness" (Romans 12:4–8).

St. Paul was addressing the congregation in Rome in the epistle quoted above, and in letters to the Corinthians, Ephesians and Colossians he sends the

† Reprinted from *The Voice of St. Jude,* (Chicago), June, 1954.

same admonition to the effect that all the faithful are under obligation to be an active part in one capacity or another of the teaching body, which is the Church.

What a large proportion of the newly converted Christians of the early centuries devoted themselves to conversation about religion and conversion of their neighbor to Christ, history makes clear in its story of the miraculous rapidity with which the faith encircled the Mediterranean and drove inland east, north and south.

The lives of patrician martyrs, converted by their slave tutors, record the technique: lay man and woman patiently breaking down accepted and established patterns of behavior by the example of truly Christian lives and then supplementing example by instruction in the doctrine, which they knew well enough to be able to explain. When Constantine, in the early fourth century, gave legal status to the Church, he found it coextensive with all civilized parts of the Empire. The next hundred years saw Christian principles written into the Empire's law and the Christian way of life supplanting pagan social customs. All of these changes, because of the very nature of reform, were, primarily, the result of the activity of the whole Christian body, and not merely the accomplishment of its very notable leaders—the Gregorys, the Cyrils, Basil, John Chrysostom, Jerome, Augustine and the rest—in whom these centuries were blessed.

The spread of the Church through the semi-civilized and barbarian sections of Europe was continued by priest and layman until it finally became the single unity of Christendom. When the dark continents were opened, at the end of the fifteenth century, the missionary orders set up "compounds," Christian villages segregated from pagan surroundings, not merely to protect the new Christians, but to set them apart that their example might serve as a living commentary on the doctrines of the Church. The rapidity of the spread of Christianity in the Americas, on the African coasts and in Portuguese Asia proves once again that the life of the Church depends jointly upon both priest and layman. Two gleaming diamonds in the crown of the Mystical Body throw light even more clear than the pages of history upon the potential force of lay action: the Japanese of Nagasaki, who preserved the faith and handed down its essential tenets for more than two hundred years, unvisited by any priest, and the Mexicans of the 1920's who emerged from mountain fastnesses where no priest had been stationed for more than a century to fight for their human rights in accordance with their Christian code.

The laity have always been apostles, otherwise the Church could not have carried out its destiny: "Go and teach." It is an age of secularism which has endowed the phrase with new popularity. When the laity were really apostles they were not self-consciously so, and they needed no underline to mark them as functioning members of the Mystical Body. The use of this phrase to separate clergy from laity is at once a symptom and a result of the secularist century which is driving a cleavage between the practice of religion and the day by day, hour by hour, living of religion, between charity and the bestowal of alms and service, between clergy and laity.

Every part of Holy Mass emphasizes the oneness of the Mystical Body. "Accept, O Holy Father, this pure, unblemished offering which I offer to atone for my countless sins, offenses and omissions, my own and of all here present; that by the mystery of this water and wine we may share" . . . "We offer this chalice" . . . "Accept us, O Lord" . . . "Accept these gifts which we bring to You" . . . "Pray, brethren, that this sacrifice, mine and yours alike," and so on throughout the Canon of the Mass. Ah, yes, the attempt at cleavage of the laity from the clergy is indeed a new and recent crime.

"It is not only the Head," wrote St. Augustine on the Mystical Body, "which has received the anointing, but also the body, and this body we are. Jesus Christ incorporates us in Himself, making us His members, that in Him we may be Christ as well." "You are a chosen race, a royal priesthood, a people God means to have for himself," wrote Saint Peter to the sojourners of the Dispersion, technically Jews outside of Palestine, but interpreted by scriptural scholars to refer to all Christians, who on earth form a dispersion from their heavenly home.

The reality of what it means to the laity to be a royal priesthood can be brought home to the individual best, it seems to the writer, by a study of what the priesthood means: first, the priesthood of Christ, the one and only Priest, our Mediator with God the

Father and Creator; second, the priesthood of those called by Him to be His ministers, His instruments, and through the sacrament of holy orders, to act in His name: "and now I am sending you out in my turn"; and, finally, the meaning of what it is to be a "priestly people." Only after such study—and there are many books written for the general reader to clarify such study—will the definition of the Christian way of life emerge, and the force of the individual Christian community, the basic cell of the Church to which all have been called to be apostles in an inseparable duality, priest and layman.

"Father, I have made thy name known to the men whom thou hast entrusted to me, chosen out of the world. I have given them my message. I have sent them into the world on my errand.

"It is not only for them that I pray; I pray for those who are to find faith in me through their word; that they may all be one; that they may too be one in us . . . so that the love thou hast bestowed upon me may dwell in them."

This is the real meaning of the apostolate of the laity. It would be a tragic thing to miss.

The Age of the Laity †

I speak to you tonight on the general subject, "The Age of the Laity."

Some time ago a noted man said, "I have felt for a very long time that if all things are to be restored in Christ, as the saintly Pius X wished, the work will have to be done, in the main, by the laity." He was right. Upon our men and women, our boys and girls, chiefly depends the well-being of Church and State, of human society at large.

They are called upon to perform a most important part in the great work of reconstruction which already confronts us all over Christendom. If they come to the rescue, all will be well; if they stand back, a fearful catastrophe is inevitable. Their intelligent, faithful and zealous cooperation is the only hope in the present crisis.

It is of no use to tell you that a reform is absolutely necessary. You see it with your own eyes. The very atmosphere in which we live brings it home to us. Naturalism, rejection of authority, mammon-worship, pleasure-mania, general hatred, open immorality, are the great evils of our age.

† Address delivered at the state convention of the Catholic Daughters of America at Worcester, Mass., May 25, 1952.

The great orator, W. Bourke Cochran of New York, told the Third Order Convention at Chicago thirty years ago: "The portentous feature of the difficult and unprecedented conditions now confronting the human family is the total inability of civilized society to cope with them. This civilization of ours, though beset by difficulties that have already arrested its progress and now threaten to overthrow it, is now literally bankrupt of resources adequate to the preservation of its existence. If we must trust to purely human agencies for relief, it is impossible to find ground on which to base a hope that the existing social order can be maintained."

At the International Lord's Day Congress in that same period Judge Alton B. Parker told his audience: "The tendency of much of the new teaching—near-religious and not near-religious—looks towards self-deification, the setting up of a little brass idol of self to adore and celebrate. New Thought, so-called, is but a new name for a cultivation of egotism that is as ancient as man. . . . We have departed a long way from the simple life of our forebears. We have fled far from the old-fashioned ideas of duty to Heaven and our neighbor. We seek to surround ourselves with luxuries—automobiles, period furniture and an infinite variety of clumsy bric-a-brac; we travel to find no culture, we read and absorb no good, we spend and spend like the proverbially intoxicated "tar," and what shall we answer when Heaven demands an account of our stewardship? We devote the precious hours and the fleeting days of our too brief opportunity in this world to petty details and selfish ends."

The words of St. Paul are surely applicable to our generation, "All seek the things that are their own, not the things that are Jesus Christ's."

In the face of this crisis, the world is honeycombed with reformers. Individuals as well as organizations are endeavoring to bring about changes for the better. We are continually hearing of new laws or other reforms which propose to cure every ill of society. Yet things are going from bad to worse. The great Pope Leo XIII indicated the right direction when he said: "Society can be healed in no other way than by a return to Christian life and Christian institutions." Unless we build on Christ and His Gospel, we build on sand. Christ lives and works in His Church. From her and through her salvation must come. But how shall the Church lead mankind back from naturalism and sin to a spiritual and religious regeneration? The falling away from God and religion came about in the face of the Church and of human society.

The origin of the religious orders may be traced to the needs of the respective periods in which they were founded. In each age, God raised the men and the means to combat the rampant evils and to uphold and protect His Church. May we expect to see another St. Francis with his Orders, another St. Ignatius and his Society? What course will divine Providence follow? Are there not clear indications that its operations have already begun, and point in another direction? Thanks be to God! Our Catholic lay forces are coming to the front. Signs of awakening are visible everywhere.

Countless men and women are gradually coming to the realization of the power for good that is in them and are exercising every means to exert it. Many a devout teacher instils solid moral principles into the plastic minds of her young charges, many a zealous nurse upholds the laws of nature's God, many a professional man and poor working man by prudence and moderation overcome prejudices, create a spirit of charity and call forth respect for religion.

The lay apostolate will bring about the transformation of human society. Its development in our age is as much the plan of divine Providence as was the origin of each religious order in its respective age. Ours is the age of the men and women who live by the Catholic faith, and whose very life is nothing but an interpretation and exemplification of the faith that is in them.

The Catholic lay apostolate, also called "Catholic Action," or "Catholic social service," in its full sense, does not mean occasional and isolated attempts, but the concerted action and united effort under the leadership of bishops and priests. It means the banding together of able and willing Catholics for the enlightenment of the ignorant, the triumph of truth, the repression of evil, the encouragement of the well-disposed, the protection of the weak, the regaining of the lost, the uplift of the downtrodden, the restoration of all in Christ. It means the reformation of Catholic life from within, and then the reformation of others by example and word and assistance. It means to become all to all in order to gain all for Christ. It is the work the apostles did centuries ago.

Catholic Daughters of America, leaders in Catholic Action, God calls you, the Church needs you, society cannot do without you. Read what the late Archbishop Goodier of Bombay had to say: "It is the inevitable consequence of the democratic age in which we live that everything—education, government, even religion, should fall into the hands of the people. There must still be schoolmasters, but the people will decide what shall be taught. There must still be ministers to frame and pass laws, but the people must tell them what these laws shall be, and see to their fulfillment. And in religion there must still be priests and bishops; there must still be all that inherited possession which no revolution can destroy; but the working element of the faith, the spread of the faith, the preservation of the faith, all this, from the very nature of the case, must devolve more and more on the people. If the people do their duty, then religion will be safe, will go forward and prosper, no matter what else may happen; if they are wanting, then no amount of preaching by its priests, or of administration by its ministers will save it from failure."

We cannot overestimate the influence you can exert on the individual and on society by promoting the works of religion, education, and charity. Some time ago an elderly gentleman of good education and wide experience, and of a keen power of observation, remarked that the influence of the priests in matters of a public nature is on the downward grade. Almost in every diocese there is a dearth of priests; on the other hand their work is steadily increasing.

The management of temporalities, official correspondence, keeping of records, conduct of social affairs, and so on—all secular functions—take up a great part of the priest's time and energy. How manifold and arduous are the sacerdotal obligations—officiating at the sacred liturgy, preaching the Word, catechizing the children, visiting the sick, instructing converts, administering the sacraments, guiding the various parish societies, conducting devotions, and many other duties.

It is very difficult to do justice to the faithful within the limits of a parish, especially if it be large and the population fleeting. Life insurance companies consider priests as poor risks. Most of them are overworked. As a rule bishops and priests can only influence those who seek their assistance. To these they can point out the way, enthuse them, encourage them, strengthen them with the grace of the sacraments, acquaint them with the dangers connected with the apostolate and thus make them their coworkers. Without the faithful cooperation of the laity, little will be accomplished in the cause of truth and holiness.

Countless opportunities not offered to the ordained minister of Christ are open to our men and women and, let me add, even our children. Their lot is cast among the people. The same problems of life confront all of them. They know existing conditions from immediate contact. Naturally, a bond of mutual interest, sympathy and friendship arises, and circles of more or less intimate acquaintances are formed. Lay apostles can quietly listen to the confidential inquiries of their friends and neighbors and unobtrusively help to solve their doubts. Such explanations are more persuasive because they are not the official utterances of the priest, but the free and spontaneous expositions of trusted friends and disinterested witnesses to the truth. More than once have I been confronted with the remark that it was very well and natural for me to speak for my Church; for that I was ordained; it was my business to do so. In years gone by I have had the happiness to instruct many converts in the faith, but I must confess that every conversion had its origin in an edifying conversation, a kind act, the friendly encouragement of some lay person, which fell quietly and imperceptibly upon the souls like a gentle dew from heaven.

So, the supreme need of the Church today is an army of earnest men and women who, imbued with the spirit of Christ, will uncompromisingly work for their religion, not so much by controversy about doctrines, but rather by the more difficult argument of a life inspired by faith and hope, and firm in its application of Christian moral principles to the common acts of daily existence. Such an army would be the very salt of democracy, and without it democracy will hardly be saved.

Pope Leo XIII wrote: "Above all, bear in mind that the indispensable condition of true zeal and the best pledge of success is purity and holiness of life." Such a life is necessarily a life of prayer.

"Those who pray," said the great statesman Donoso Cortes, "do more for the world than those who fight; and if the world is growing worse, it is because there are more battles than prayers." And Bossuet tells us that the hands raised heavenward overcome more enemies than those that strike. Of ourselves we are nothing and can do nothing, yet each of us should be able to say in the spirit of humility with St. Paul: "Be ye followers of me, as I am also of Christ." Prayer is an essential duty. Without it we cannot be true Christians, still less "the light of the world" and "the salt of the earth." Our sufficiency is from God. Only the Christian of fervent and incessant prayer has the spirit of Christ and can communicate it to others.

Although our Lord's mission was to save souls, He spent thirty years of His life in recollection and solitude, and made a retreat of forty days as a prelude to His evangelical career of only three years. In the course of His apostolic ministry He frequently withdrew into desert places in order to pray. "He spent the night in prayer." He intended to show us by His own example the importance of prayer in the work of salvation. "Seeing the multitudes, He had compassion on them; because they were distressed, and lying like sheep that have no shepherd. Then He saith to His disciples, 'The harvest indeed is great, but the laborers are few'." The only remedy He gives for the sad dearth of workers is prayer. "Pray ye, therefore, the Lord of the harvest, that he send forth laborers into his harvest." If the mere supplication of pious souls is preferable to anything else as a means of supplying laborers, it follows that the fruitfulness of any undertaking for the benefit of souls depends principally on prayer.

When Mary was quietly sitting at the feet of Jesus

and listening to His words, He said to the busy and complaining Martha: "Martha, Martha, thou art careful, and art troubled about many things; but one thing is necessary. Mary hath chosen the best part." The spirit of prayer is the best part; it will produce the most desirable results. The apostles followed our Savior. They reserved to themselves, in the first place, the office of prayer and then the ministry of the word. "But we will give ourselves continually to prayer, and to the ministry of the word." First prayer, then preaching.

The Little Flower of Jesus used to quote the following from Archimedes: "Give me a lever and a fulcrum on which to lean it, and I will lift the world." She then continues: "What he could not obtain because his request had only a material end, without reference to God, the saints have obtained in all its fullness. They lean on God Almighty's power itself and their lever is the prayer that inflames with love's fire. With this lever they have raised the world—with this lever the saints of the Church militant still raise it, and will raise it to the end of time."

The apostolate of prayer is within the capacity of all, and it can be exercised at all times, amidst all kinds of occupations, even during sickness, when other works of zeal are impossible . . .

Filled, then, with the spirit of prayer, you will be ready for your place in the apostolate. That place I have told you many times. Pope Pius X one day, while conversing with some cardinals, asked them: "What is most necessary for the welfare of contemporary society?" "To build schools," replied one.

"No," answered the Holy Father. "To increase the number of churches," another said. Again the Pope disagreed. "To secure more vocations to the priesthood," ventured a third one. The Supreme Pontiff disagreed with this also and replied: "The most urgent need of the day is to form in every parish a group of lay people who are well informed, resolute and courageous—who are truly apostles."

No matter who you are, you should be an apostle. If you take your religion seriously, you will desire to do something for Christ. His love will urge you. Every day the world grows larger and more open, and there are more souls to be saved or brought nearer to God. Never before in the history of the human race has the Christian who would be an apostle had such an opportunity as now. What can you do? Allow me to give you some suggestions.

Besides praying, practicing mortifications, and giving a good example, you surely want to exercise the apostolate of humble, kind, and firm words and actions. If you would be able to satisfy the minds of those with whom you mingle, you must be well informed about your religion. Hence the first requisite is careful study. Are you in a position to point out, to explain, and prove the divine institution of the Church, and the conformity of her teachings to sound reason and divine revelation? Have you the right conception of her practices and ordinances? What use are you making of books that contain wholesome and practical instruction, of pamphlets and papers that treat on the bearings of our faith on the questions of the day, of a literature that will ground you more firmly in the principles of your holy religion?

It is to help you answer these questions as an apostle should that the Catholic Daughters of America study club program has been inaugurated. I pray that it is flourishing in all your courts. I trust that it will be intensified.

Are you the friends of youth? The rising generation will dominate the world. Socialists, rationalists, communists are making their strongest bid for the souls of children, frequently of our children. If we would promote the Kingdom of Christ on earth we must at all times be unqualified in our interest in, unstinted in our generosity to whatever programs enlist the loyalty and enhance the lives of young people. That is why the Catholic Daughters have placed such great hopes in their Junior program. I pray that this is flourishing. I trust that it will continue to do so. Are you a loyal member of your own parish? The good parishioner's heart is attached to her parish. It is through her parish that she is united with the diocese and with the universal Church. The parish church is the spiritual home of each Christian. She seeks to serve it in a spirit of humility and generosity. That is why the Catholic Daughters of America have always tried to make their members lively and loyal parishioners. I hope that this emphasis will always be strong in the Order. Are your courts closely identified with the interests of your individual dioceses? If they are not, then they are not working in the spirit of the Catholic Daughters of America, for theirs is traditionally a spirit of close dependence on and fidelity to the bishops of the Catholic Church. Finally, is each one of you striving to be individually an apostle? If not, the Catholic Daughters of America have not done for you singly what the Order exists to do: namely, prepare you to be an apostle even if there were no one else to help you.

Sometimes you will ask: "What can I do alone?" The history of the Church is the answer. It is not numbers but willingness, not learning but self-sacrifice; not even any special skill or training, but a strong desire to do good, a strong hand to put to the plough. That not mere numbers make the difference, the past has clearly shown. Newman says well: "Moses was one, Elias was one, David was one, Leo was one, Athanasius was one. Grace ever works by the few. It is the keen vision, the intense conviction, the indomitable resolve of the few. It is the blood of the martyr, it is the prayer of the saint, it is the heroic deed, it is the momentary crisis, it is the concentrated energy of a look or a word which is the instrument of heaven." I pray God that you will each be an instrument of heaven, a spiritual mother as well as a Catholic Daughter of America.

The Vocation of the Laity †

"For you have been reborn not from corruptible seed but from incorruptible through the word of God who lives and abides forever" (*I Peter 1:23*).

A little more than a month ago Pope Pius XII spoke to the College of Cardinals these forceful and profoundly challenging words:

"Today many turn in anxious expectancy and trembling hope to the Church. The Church must respond to this hope, and so must reject any false concept of her spirituality which would confine her to the retirement of the sanctuary. The Church must fulfill her divinely providential mission of forming the complete man and of collaborating in the construction of the solid foundations of society. In this work of the Church, the laity must not stand idly by. Our laity do not merely belong to the Church: they are the Church and must take their stand in the front line of its life."

Timely words these, and dictated at once by the spirit of God and the needs of the hour. This is not the first time that the Church has been called upon to do her work of regeneration in a society bankrupt

† Sermon delivered on the occasion of the conferring of the pallium on the Archbishop in the Cathedral of the Holy Cross, Boston, April 7, 1946.

except for the hope that springs eternal in the human spirit. The Graeco-Roman world which confronted the apostolic ages was far closer to despair than is our age. Religion and morality were at ebb tide. The Scriptures give us the picture. When Peter looked over the field of his mission, he could see only dissipation, lust, drunkenness, perversion, and unlawful worship of idols. The religious revolution through which the pagan world had lived for three centuries had left the leaders agnostics and atheists. Although the masses could still cry, "Great is Diana of the Ephesians," it was more a rallying cry for their distorted, corrupt rites than a religious uplifting of their hearts to the supernatural.

Yet it was not in despair but in buoyant confidence that the little band of disciples set forth to carry the word of salvation to mankind. Then, as now, many were turning in anxious expectancy to the teachings of Christ. Few in number, but stronger than a multitude through the power of that Holy Spirit, these humble followers of Christ taught Christ crucified, His justice and His charity, the systematic imitation of His Life, which would have for its infallible effect the personal rebirth of the individual and the radical reformation of any society in which he lived. Thus St. Paul could write:

"You became imitators of us and of the Lord, receiving the word in great tribulation, with the joy of the Holy Spirit, so that you became a pattern to all believers in Macedonia and Achaia."

Following the commandments and the counsels of Christ, the early Christian laity became a nucleus of promise for the unity of a divided world and the hope of a desperate society. By the second century, a pro-consul, writing to the Roman emperor for instructions on how to deal with Christians, acknowledged that their whole life appeared to have for its purpose the practice of charity and the fulfillment of justice. "See these Christians, how they love one another."

Thus Saint Paul could also write:

"Concerning brotherly charity, there is no need for us to write to you, for you yourselves have learned from God to love one another." Surely love of neighbor was then no idle phrase in the personal and social pattern of the Catholic laity.

From the beginning of Christendom the commandments of justice went side by side with those of love in the formation of the laity and in their reformation of the world. How specifically they applied these, what a social revolution they wrought, we can learn from the writings of apostolic times. "To all men their due," wrote St. Peter, "to the brethren your love, to God your reverence, to the king due honor." The Apostle of the Gentiles advised all men to work that they might walk becomingly toward outsiders and need nothing themselves. And St. James rebuked those who would keep back the pay of the workingman. The poor—those we now call the unemployed—and the weak and the ignorant became the charges of society, that is to say, of the rich, for the rich held their wealth only in stewardship. Slave and master were taught their mutual obligations, and a society in which the lowly had been as truly "untouchable" as India's pariahs today, slowly gave place to a Christian order realizing the same religious standards which Pius XII holds up anew when he pleads in our day for a society of "men, established in their inviolable integrity as images of God, proud of their personal dignity, jealous of their equality with their fellows in all that touches the essential bases of man's dignity." The hierarchy and the priesthood taught the principles of that society, but it was the laity who built, in patient perseverance and undying faith, its foundations and its fabric!

"For you have been reborn not from corruptible seed but from incorruptible through the Word of God who lives and abides forever."

There is a sense in which the history of the Church is the history of the vicar of Christ and of the hierarchy and other clergy who help govern the Church. But our natural preoccupation with the accomplishments of the Church's leaders should not cause us to forget that the history of the spread and influence of the Church in secular society is largely the story of the laity, of apostolic men and women.

In the early chronicles of Christianity we read over and over again the challenge to the laity to spread the faith by action, by example, and by teaching. "Do you think that Scripture means nothing," thundered St. James, "when it tells you that the Spirit dwells in you, loves you with a jealous love?" "Would you have faith and no deeds to show for it?" "Faith without works is dead!" And, even more strongly, he wrote, "If a man has the power to do good, it is sinful for him to leave it undone."

In very truth, the devout laity of the primitive Church were the citizens of heaven; yet they were also the soul of the world. Like contemplatives, the apostolic laity devoted themselves to prayer; like active religious, they practiced their almsdeeds; and they studied and instructed others in the faith.

Countless converts were made by lay Christians who instructed those with whom they were associated in pagan society. In the great persecutions uncounted numbers of the laity took their places beside the bishops and priests who sealed with their blood their loyalty to their Lord. The great ages of faith, nourished by their martyrdoms, were not ages of faith in the monasteries and sanctuaries alone; they were ages of faith on every level of society, in every sphere of human action. No one then thought of the faith as a departmental thing, or as the characteristic of a class or a caste. It was the equal and common possession of priests and people, of clergy and laity.

How different the picture in our day! In spite of the great prominence of religion in the news, and in spite of the truly impressive activity of the devout, we can point to large areas of civilization in which there are multitudes living without God. Not only has revelation been assailed on all sides, but millions have lost the very idea of a Day of Judgment and a life to come; their whole reasoning and practice take for granted the Epicurean maxim: "Live today; there is no tomorrow."

Religion was once a great public authority known to all, which could not be overlooked or put away; it had the support of the law and made its power felt;

nor would anyone have dreamt of calling it a matter for the private conscience alone. But now, all too often and almost everywhere, it is something which stands at a distance from the daily business of the people; they may take it or leave it, and coercion is a thing of the past. Even some churchmen are occasionally heard to applaud this phenomenon which seems to us religious liberalism run riot.

Owing to these and other circumstances, which affect everyone, religion tends to become a cloistered art—a profession of which the sphere is the church, the school, the convent, but which has little or no direct bearing on the world at large. When the layman has done with school or college, too frequently he has done with religion. He passes into a society as unlike that of which his teachers have spoken to him as if it were on a different planet. If he continues to be devout, still his duties appear to be fulfilled when he has received the sacraments and made certain contributions to his pastor. What public duties, besides these, did he ever learn in his young days? The conception of a social Christianity, here and now to be realized—who has taught him that? The parish—what is it, too often, but a name, identical with the four walls of the building within which he hears his Sunday Mass or received his Easter Communion? The Church itself, in our modern condition of life, is not visible, but invisible. Outside and all around about is the great world, and its atmosphere, I repeat, is indifferentism and secularism.

The consequences of all this should be clearly understood. Christians, by their baptism and by the vow they have taken at confirmation, are soldiers of Christ, apostles to those that do not believe, and citizens of the Gospel kingdom. All alike, men and women, have rights within the Church, and therefore duties to themselves, to one another, to strangers. But how few, in comparison, escape the taint of secular indifference, once they leave our schools.

For the restoration of the laity to their proper place in the life and the Catholic Action of the Church, we have given every possible encouragement to the organization of our laymen and women, and we shall continue to do so. We have tried to demonstrate the conviction of our hierarchy that in the Catholic Church there is, and ought to be, a lay apostolate. It is not enough to say one's prayers, receive the sacraments, and help to support one's pastor. These are all necessary; but these are not sufficient. Catholicism has never considered that the fullness of Catholic life consists in keeping the six precepts of the Church. Something more positive is required.

When the Church has raised to her altars devout laymen, it is remarkable that the most illustrious among them have held public offices, and did large social service in their day and generation. The heroic leaders of the past were such as St. Edward, St. Henry, St. Louis, St. Thomas More. Others held in grateful remembrance, examples to us all were such as O'Connell, Montalembert, Ozanam, Brownson, Louis Pasteur, the Prince of Science; William George Ward, the scholarly defender of the Faith—names eminent in politics which were not partisan, names eminent in learning that was not narrowing but liberating and humanitarian, names written high on the crusade of piety and of social action inspired by the deepest principles of the Christian religion. From historic instances like these, which might be multiplied indefinitely, it is clear that laymen may and should exert a most effective and beneficial influence all round them as Catholic apostles. The principle is beyond dispute; examples are abundant; yet I ask whether in our schools and colleges we make sufficient mention of these things, and how far we do what in us lies to kindle an enthusiasm which, bye and bye, shall find scope and utterance in societies adapted to its working.

This work of teaching the social Christian creed should begin at school. But it should not end there! It must be followed up in every parish, in every group by appropriate channels for the Church's formation of an instructed laity.

If adult education be the answer, then the laity must have religion classes and parish guilds and ample opportunity to enjoy guidance in pursuing, in well-chosen books, a sure knowledge of theology, an acquaintance with the spiritual life, and an understanding of the Church's social teachings as these are expounded by the popes and their commentators. To the partial fulfillment of this end, we have recently inaugurated the Confraternity of Christian Doctrine in the Archdiocese, and we have invited to Boston the Eighth National Congress of the Confraternity.

We can be pardonably proud of the devotional life of our people. Nowhere in modern times have the laity in such large numbers come out from their houses in the dark hours of winter mornings to attend the daily Sacrifice of the Mass and to receive Holy Communion. They crowd the churches for benediction, hours of adoration, novena services; practically all are equally faithful to their Sunday Mass and sacramental obligations; they support their parishes generously and they give joyously to the works of education and charity. But we must honestly question how much of this devotion proceeds from good hearts and loyal wills, and how much springs from mature intellectual faith.

The hour has come for us to cease to expect a child's study of a child's catechism to give an adult's appreciation of an essentially intellectual religion. The effort to attain the intellectual vision, the clear thinking and the moral integrity for which the Holy Father calls, can be based only on a systematic study by the laity of the principles of justice and charity as they apply to modern problems of life and thought. Only then will the world that looks to the Church with ever more anxious expectancy be given grounds for hope. Then others will be inspired to collaborate with us on a Christian basis, and some of these will join the ranks of the Church. The march of converts is uninterrupted. I have confirmed 2500 of them within the last year at this altar rail alone. A laity that knows its faith cannot fail to be fired by the desire to share it with others; a laity so inspired cannot but move others to seek the faith. The statistics of any parish will show that it is rarely that a person really studies the faith without ultimately seeking baptism.

Mission territory tells the same story. The countries that refuse the faith take care to forbid its teaching.

One of the most distinguished converts of our time is Dr. John Wu, fellow-countryman of one of the great prelates who honors us by being present today. Dr. Wu was associated with a cultured Catholic Chinese group of Shanghai. Many of them were praying for his conversion. A great legal authority, at one time offered a place on the Harvard faculty of Comparative Law, Dr. Wu had spent many years in the United States. One night at the home of a friend he picked up the autobiography of the Little Flower of Jesus. He returned radiant the next day. "If Thérèse of Lisieux represents the Catholic religion," he exclaimed, "then I must become a Catholic." It is sad to think of the tens of thousands in our own country who, like Dr. Wu, would find in the Church the home they are seeking, if we but reached out a hand to them and if, like the Christians of old, we led lives that shone in contrast to the pale indifference, the uninspired secularism and the cold materialism of the world about us.

It is frequently observed that our age is not unlike that which confronted the primitive Church. I have tried to suggest just that, and to argue that the remedy must be sought in a re-inspired laity like to those who were the co-workers of the apostles. But the Church is in a better position today than she was then to contribute to a spiritually bankrupt society the principles of eternal wisdom and the technique of reconstruction. Under the same divine Guide who led her to the conquest of ancient paganism, under the incomparable leadership of our Holy Father, Pope Pius XII; with a newly-constituted College of Cardinals representing every facet of Catholic thought and able to interpret each his own country's wants and needs, she can save civilization and reestablish the City of God if we, her own, do not betray her by indifference, by ignorance, by inaction and inertia.

Today, as in the Graeco-Roman world, the need and the remedy are spiritual; in that world there were no traditions and few customs with the aid of which the Christians could work; but today the fragments of the torn and broken world are at least Christian fragments. Justice and charity were their weapons of reconstruction; so too are they ours. The Vicar of Christ has called us to action, priests and laity alike. The action must be unified, corporate, completely cooperative. That is why I have chosen this day, when representatives of every parish of the Archdiocese of Boston are gathered here, when we have received the symbol of our unity with the Sovereign Pontiff, to speak of the apostolate of the laity, of your unity with me in the work of our archdiocese. Our vocation is to be, so near as human frailty permits, blameless shepherds; yours is to be a militant, untiring, undaunted flock. The challenge of the age is awe-inspiring; but be not discouraged:

"For you have been reborn not from corruptible seed but from incorruptible through the Word of God who lives and abides forever."

Two

SANCTITY AND LAY APOSTLES

Sanctity and the Laity †

A divine discontent led Christopher Columbus to seek the new continent. A divine faith in himself and in Almighty God led him to find it.

Columbus was a Catholic, a fervent Catholic, one whose intense spirituality admits of no doubt. The influence of his religion upon his life-work was of a paramount character. A non-Catholic authority declares that the virtue of piety "ran through all his life, attended him on every occasion, cheered him in his trials, comforted him in his bodily afflictions, illumined the vision he caught of the world's redemption, and closed his eyes in final faith."

It was well that the discoverer was gifted with extraordinary spirituality. The obstacles which beset him for long years in his endeavors to gain the cooperation of those in high places for his undertaking were neither light nor easily borne. Success rewarded his efforts in 1492, when the Spanish sovereigns, Ferdinand and Isabella, acquiesced in his plans.

Knights of Columbus, you have not been called, like Columbus of old, to discover a new continent

† Sermon given at the annual corporate Mass and Communion of the State Council, Knights of Columbus, in Holy Cross Cathedral, Boston, October 13, 1952.

but as brothers in the same faith, you are called to follow the way of heroic sanctity.

The most urgent need of our times is sanctity. The particular call to Catholic men in our generation is the call for sanctity. There is no greater contribution you can make, either to the Church or to the general society, than that of heroic holiness.

We read of the saints of yesteryear, of the heroic souls in centuries gone by who died as martyrs, labored as confessors, sacrificed as virgins, sanctified the world as saints and made manifest in their own flesh the holiness that is the secret strength of the Church. We know the names of these saints. We need merely repeat our litanies to recall them by scores. But are they not all of the past and do not their very names suggest how far were their lives and their luster from our shores and our times? What of holiness in our own day?

There is something of the saint in every contemplative or else he would never enter upon a life so secret and so holy. But there is also something of the contemplative in every saint, for sanctity effaces itself, seeks to hide itself. Even the saints whose vocation or destiny keeps them in the world somehow manage to surround their sanctity with a kind of cloister. Sanctity by its very nature is the least obvious of the marks of the Church and yet by no mark is the Church kept so close to Christ and made so intimately His as by its holiness.

We can only discover with difficulty our contemporary saints, while the saints of yore are familiar to us. But so it has always been; the saints whose names and fame are the public property of our generation were hidden souls in the days when they walked the earth, their holiness unknown to most of those among whom they then lived. Alexis, a despised beggar in his own father's house, was recognized for a saint only when he was cold in death. Many are the saints who were persecuted and accused of all manner of evil while they were alive, persecuted even by some who esteemed themselves and were esteemed by others as just. Their victims were acknowledged as saints long after death had claimed them. Could any example be more plain than that of Joan of Arc?

Today's saint is always yesterday's despised prophet, repudiated fool or unknown friend of God. Tomorrow's saints are on earth today; their sanctity hidden, unrecognized or cloistered. But I am convinced that our generation is extremely productive of saints, more so doubtless than any other period of Christian history. What is even more wonderful and even more easily proved: our saints are found on every level of this generation's life, especially among laymen.

Holiness is still dramatically exemplified by the missionaries of the Church, particularly at the moment when they are dying bloody or bloodless martyrdoms, but it is far from limited to them. If it were, there would be no purpose in the plea which I make to you today. All of us, without exception, are called to holiness. Under the circumstances in which our generation lives and works, that holiness must be heroic, but in pursuit of it you have abundant examples among the laity of modern times. I think it well to remind you of them as you gather to honor a man of heroic sanctity.

All ages are represented, all classes of society are among the laymen of heroic sanctity whom the Church has produced in modern times. A veritable litany could be composed of your lay brethren whose lives demonstrate how Christ is ardently loved and served in this age so frequently labeled "godless." They are proofs that in an unbelieving, restless and perverse world, oases of sanctity still exist.

Sometimes you may think that total night has overtaken us. Lift up your heads. Countless golden points pierce the darkness; the night is alive with stars.

Within the year there was published a book by a French priest whose long life has been given up almost entirely to the spiritual direction of young men. His priest-career long made him the confidant of university men, soldiers, young married men, beginners in the professions and in the working classes. His contacts with young men covered three full generations; he has known intimately men of your age in two centuries, the nineteenth and the twentieth.

Against this rich background of experience the old priest did not hesitate to say that Christian heroism, heroic sanctity, is currently achieved by greater numbers of young men than have sought or attained it at any other time within memory. He asserts that the scores of young men, whose lives of heroic sanctity he recounts in his book, are but a few of the legions he could personally cite. I believe that he is right.

When it comes to the mature Catholic men of our

generation, the evidences of heroic holiness which this experienced author presents are truly extraordinary. In France, Belgium, Germany and Italy alone he is able to name of his personal knowledge numerous industrialists, statesmen, professional men, army officers, university professors and scientists whose lives are characterized by heroic holiness.

His book records impressions like to those of any priest whose experience with souls has penetrated beneath the surface of society. A wise confessor once remarked: "People lament that there are no more saints! As for me, I find them wherever I go." It is nowhere more true than here in America. Believe one who knows.

The heroic sanctity which I assert is the need of the hour, a need which I further assert that the Catholic Church is meeting, shows up in the most surprising places. On Sunday, June 7, 1925, a workman dies suddenly in a Dublin street. Under his clothes are found instruments of penance which have eaten into his very flesh. Who is this mysterious man? He is a humble worker. For forty years he has practiced austerities reminiscent of the legends of the hermits of old. From two o'clock in the morning he has prayed like a monk. As soon as the churches are opened, he hears Mass until it is time for work. He takes his meals kneeling. None had known the full extent of his sanctity during his lifetime. He dies. Interest is aroused. Within six months following the publication of a sketch of his life, twenty thousand copies have been bought up by other workers. The name of this workman: Matt Talbot.

In the midst of a generation of petty crime and sensuality, here is a further reminder of the vitality of the Church that produced a host of humble saints in centuries past.

At the other end of the social ladder, in 1940 a visitor to a monastery in central France is amazed to see a familiar face among the monks who are chanting matins and lauds in the small hours of the morning. He makes inquiries and finds that the layman has been a retreatant at the monastery for two full weeks of each year for many years past. Upon further inquiry he discovers something of the other spiritual practices of the man whose face he recognized. He learns about his penitential austerities and his extraordinary vigils of prayer. He had hitherto known him only as one of the outstanding diplomats of the day, a layman whose name is a household word and whose personal holiness is almost completely unknown, save to a few trusted friends.

In a period of widely publicized abuse of office, here is a reminder of the continuing power to sanctify of the Church that gave us St. Thomas More and King St. Louis.

The tides of battle roll backward and forward between the Allies and the Central Powers in World War I. Among the soldiers who die is a young lieutenant, killed as soon as he reaches the front. In his hand there is the pistol that Caesar bade him carry. In his knapsack they find a spiritual diary revealing the heroic holiness which the Church had given him. It is the document of a saint—and the spiritual reflections of that soldier have ever since served as the inspiration of only God knows how many thousands of young soldiers.

We are frequently told of the tendency of military life to corrupt. Here is a proof that for some it can be a means to holiness. A famed playwright, recently deceased, was a profligate until he entered military service. There he was converted by the manifest holiness of his lieutenant.

We hear so much of the evil geniuses of our day: of the dictators, the racketeers, the perverse and the traitorous. It is well that we recall occasionally the other side of the ledger, and that as you go forth into the world of business, of professional life, soldiery and politics, you be aware of the multitude of laymen who live the faith, the faith by which you, too, can be brought to heroic sanctity.

As a counteractive to all that the daily papers tell you of human ingenuity in evil, I urge you to make it your business to read the lives of modern men who have had holiness for their ambition. The stories of Frederick Ozanam, of Thomas More, of Matt Talbot, of the martyrs in Mexico a quarter century ago and those in the East today, will remind you that God is not dead; that His Church has not lost its power to produce saints; and that the dawn may be nearer than we think.

Then you will better appreciate the place that holiness must have both in your personal lives and in the life of our generation. We constantly hear of the need for ideas and of the need for action. Both needs are real and both are urgent. But still more necessary is the need for sanctity. That is what the anguish of the present day requires above all else. The world demands saints.

Christian heroism, a heroic holiness among men, is the one and only solution of the problems of life. It is precisely when the state of human history seems worst that God pours forth His most abundant graces and prepares for the richest harvest of holiness.

It is my conviction that such a harvest is in preparation among us—and that this period of history will see more sanctity among the laity than any other century has hitherto been privileged to witness.

Do not believe those who tell you that saints are becoming more and more rare. Do not believe those who suggest that the sources of sanctity are running thin, that the Church is spiritually sick and no longer producing her saints. I repeat: Sometimes we think the night has totally overtaken us. But lift up your heads! Countless are the lives whose flaming sanctity throngs like stars in the midst of darkness.

Ours is the age of the saints, of saintly priests and saintly nuns, but above all of laymen seeking heroic sanctity. I pray God that the Knights of Columbus will be leaders among them!

Personal Sanctification †

The theme of this holy hour is the most important single question that could possibly be proposed for discussion.

It is concerned with what Jesus of Nazareth called "the one thing necessary," the only thing which matters when all is said and done: the salvation of my individual soul.

Social reform, economic prosperity, political order, cultural growth, even the prosperity of the Church herself are all secondary to this supreme, uniquely important problem: the salvation of the individual soul of every man here present.

Salvation is the fruit of personal sanctification—and therefore there is nothing we could possibly discuss more important than personal sanctification.

"What does it profit a man to gain the whole world and suffer the loss of his own soul?"

When Jesus Christ threw down that question as a challenge to the world, He was saying in effect that no social, political, economic or ecclesiastical problem can be anything more than secondary as contrasted with the question of personal sanctification.

What does it profit a man to conquer the whole

† Address delivered to 45,000 men assembled at a religious rally in Fenway Park, Boston, September 27, 1953.

world and impose upon it a universal order of peace—and then be damned himself for lack of personal sanctification?

What does it profit a man to teach the world the riddle of the universe, the sum of all knowledge—and then be damned for failing to learn the secret of personal sanctification?

What does it profit a man to govern the whole world or any part thereof with wisdom, prudence and prosperous effect—and then be damned because, although possessed of a gift for social and collective administration, he lacked the disciplines of personal sanctification?

It is God's will that we strive for international, national and local order. It is God's will that we achieve a maximum measure of the refinement of the mind by culture, the perfection of the body by health, the flourishing of human institutions in prosperity and peace. All these things are God's will. But they are secondary objectives in God's plan. The primary will of God, the supreme and essential will of God, is the theme of this holy hour: the personal sanctification of each one of us.

"This is the will of God," says St. Paul, "your sanctification!"

St. Paul time and again hammers at this idea that personal sanctification is the essence of the Christian life, the one indispensable requirement without which all else is vain, empty and pointless.

It is of personal sanctification that St. Paul was speaking when he wrote his uncompromising, blunt words about the emptiness of all save charity.

You remember what he said: suppose I were a genius at languages and could speak to all men in their own tongues, persuading them with the inspiration of an angel; what wonders I would accomplish for God, for society, for the Church, for men! And yet, without personal sanctification I would still be damned. I would be better off deaf, dumb and blind, but sanctified personally, than I would be with the eloquence of men and angels but lacking personal sanctification.

Suppose I had the mind of a genius, so keen, so talented, so marvelously endowed that I knew things past by erudition, things present by intuition and experience, things to come by prophecy. What power would then be mine! And yet, again I would be damned if, having all wisdom and prophecy, I lacked personal sanctification.

Suppose something even more startling, perhaps even incredible. Suppose I had faith so great that I could work miracles; suppose I were so generous and so zealous that my days and nights were consumed in the service of the poor; suppose I exhausted myself in good works—but neglected personal sanctification. My neighbors would benefit. The community would be stronger. The Church might even prosper because of my accomplishments. But I would be damned.

"What does it profit a man to gain the whole world and suffer the loss of his own soul?" What does it profit a man, as Paul also warned, to preach the gospel of salvation to all others and yet become himself an outcast by defect of personal sanctification?

In a sense which every Christian understands, it makes no difference what becomes of the world and all things in it. The world of things is well lost, if I save my soul. The societies we sweat so to pacify and promote—secular and religious alike—are ultimately important only to the extent that they help each of us save his soul. Political institutions are ultimately important only because they insure conditions of freedom and prosperity which facilitate personal growth, and above all the growth which is personal sanctification. The gospel itself and the mighty Church which Jesus founded are means to an end greater than themselves, sublime though they be, and that end is the personal sanctification of every soul.

Your theme is wisely chosen, then, and nothing could be more important. In times past I have summoned you to collective Catholic Action. In times to come I shall call upon you, as would any shepherd of the Christian flock, to support and to be active in the organized programs of religion and in the spiritual regeneration of society. All of this is important; none of it may be neglected. But something else is more important and nothing, not even these other things to which you are bound to give your aid, can come between you and the one thing necessary, the most important thing: the salvation of your individual soul by personal sanctification.

If all our organizations were to disintegrate; if all our collective programs were to be driven underground; if society itself collapsed in anarchy and the soul of each man here present were saved through personal sanctification, no one of us would regret the price. "What does it profit a man to gain the whole world and suffer the loss of his own soul?" "This is the will of God, your sanctification!"

All this may sound too selfish, too individualistic or too self-centered to be good Christian doctrine. You may think: "How can a man save his own soul if he disregards the fate of the group to which he belongs? How can there be personal sanctification without social responsibility? Is not every man bound to make the world about him better as the condition of his own self-salvation and personal sanctification? Do we not have a redeeming part to play in the world about us, a contribution to make to the spread of the kingdom of God and the strengthening of His Church—and are not all these required of us quite as much as is solicitude for our personal well-being, our personal sanctification included?"

The answer to all these questions is a simple one. Personal sanctification is the supreme business of life, and far from being inconsistent with these other social and group responsibilities, it is the principal means to their fulfillment, too. When I sanctify myself, I accomplish my chief duty, the salvation of my soul, but I also make my principal contribution, though not my only one, to the good order of the societies to which I belong, both secular and religious.

So basic is this truth that, having reminded you that personal sanctification is ultimately all that matters, I now assert that personal sanctification is the beginning and the corner-stone of all social regeneration, political reform and the right ordering of the Church herself.

The primacy of personal self-sanctification is something which St. Francis of Assisi understood perfectly and preached unforgettably. Let me tell you a story about him. It is a timely story because the generation in which St. Francis lived was a generation threatened by evils like those which threaten us.

In the days when St. Francis was young, the pope in Rome was sorely perplexed by the state of the Church and the confusion of the times. He listened carefully to the advice of his most eminent counselors and he turned in desperation to all the wisest and most experienced of advisers. Bewildered by conflicting counsel, disturbed by the Church's problems, one night the pope, in troubled sleep, dreamed a strange dream. He saw the great cathedral of his own city, St. John Lateran, tottering before the onslaught of hostile winds; the great cathedral, the head and the mother of all the churches of Christendom, despite its massive columns and its reinforced ramparts, seemed a house of sand in the face of the tempest which threatened it. And then he saw a man come running, a small man, seemingly timid and inconsequential. The dreaming pontiff watched the small man place his hand against the trembling walls of the cathedral and by his touch steady it and restore it to stability. He saw the man of his dream fall to work and rebuild to even greater strength and beauty the great temple, a symbol of the Church itself, which in the opening visions of his sleep had seemed forever doomed.

The next morning, legend tells us, there came to the Holy Father a small man like the man in his dream. It was Francis of Assisi. Humble in outward aspect, soft-spoken and mild, the strange man had an amazing request to make. He asked the permission of the Holy Father to begin the titanic work of reconstructing Christendom, of reforming the Church in all its wayward members and restoring to the city of God on earth its beauty, influence and prestige. This was the hope of the Holy Father himself, but before he could give such a permission, he addressed to the little man of Assisi this question: "How can this be done, how can you accomplish it?"

Francis answered: "I propose to rebuild the Church of God by following Jesus Christ in a spirit of simplicity and purity." And thus there began the great Franciscan movement, inspired by God, espoused by a host of holy souls from every class and condition of men, encouraged by Church authority on every level, beginning and ending with the vicar of Christ himself. Once, seven centuries ago, when Europe and Christendom seemed doomed, the world was renewed and its institutions were purified by that simple formula.

The formula of St. Francis—"simplicity and purity"—is another way of saying personal sanctification. His promise to rebuild the Church itself by such a formula is another way of saying that the personal sanctification of individuals is the only way to social reform.

The Church in our generation teaches the same clear and saving formula. Her trumpet sounds no uncertain note. Her code is consistent; it requires today no more, no less than it required yesterday, than it required a century, ten centuries, two thousand years ago. Her creed is as unchanging and as unmistakable as that Christ who is its core; yesterday, today, forever the same.

What do you wish to ask of her? Do you seek the principles which make for social peace? She need call no convention, conduct no symposium, subsidize no commission to devise her answer. She heard it first in the Sermon on the Mount from the lips of God Himself; she has not changed a syllable of it since. It is personal sanctification.

Do you seek the formula by which family life can be made at once sane and saintly? She need call upon no specialists, themselves bewildered and at sea, to offer you the formula you seek; no prolonged experiments, no contradictory case studies need delay her in reaching her conclusions. She found the formula for family life at Nazareth, in the personal sanctification of Joseph, a conscientious worker whose character the Scriptures summarize in the single word: just; in the personal sanctification of Mary, a chaste mother whom an angel of God Himself was obliged to hail as "full of grace."

Do you seek a pattern for self-development, for individual happiness, for the integration of your personal life? The Church need not send you to some new prophet of a philosophy untried and insecure. Two thousand years ago she heard from Him who lived the only perfect life our race has seen, the means to all that earth or heaven can teach you of perfection. "If thou wilt be perfect . . . come follow me!" "Learn of me for I am meek and humble of heart."

That formula boils down to personal sanctification.

Thus clear, unqualified and unchanging are the formulas which the Church offers those who turn to her for guidance in this our day. The world presents no such clarity, consistency nor calm. Time after time within the memory of living man satanic floods of human blood have not sufficed to wash out the monuments to the failure of our secular civilization to devise a formula for political peace. The civic prophets of our society use words which are ancient and honorable, words which inflame the human heart and inspire men to sacrifices which are heroic in their purpose but pathetic in their result.

Words like democracy, social justice, liberty, brotherhood, tolerance, freedom from fear, freedom from want—all these catchwords of our secular civilization are brave words and challenging, but no two statesmen, no two teachers, no two citizens who use them mean the same things by them. And few there are or none who are prepared to tell us how to achieve the values without which these words are empty sounds.

Seven centuries ago the pope of Rome, appalled by confusion in Christendom, saw a small man come running in his dream and steady by the mere touch of his strong hand the trembling walls of the City of God. The pope awoke to hear St. Francis, the man of his dreams, recall the ancient formula by which his steadying hands acquired their strength: "I propose to rebuild the Church of God by following Jesus

Christ in simplicity and purity, by walking in His footsteps wherever His steps may lead." In obedience to that formula, that is, by personal sanctification, we —you and I—can rebuild the walls of our world—and at the same time save our souls.

St. Francis said: "I propose to rebuild the Church of God by following Jesus Christ in the spirit of simplicity and purity." Once when the world was being torn apart by hatreds and all things had grown grey with cynicism, that inspired formula of our saint, echoed in the hearts of millions, brought back peace to divided nations and prosperity to broken homes. God grant that it may do so once again! There is no other remedy for the evils of our day. There is no substitute for Jesus Christ. We become like to Him through personal sanctification. By it we gain heaven. By it we renew the face of the earth. I charge you: make good, each of you, the slogan of your rally.

Faith, Hope and Charity—Spurs to Catholic Action †

"Except you eat the flesh of the Son of Man and drink His blood, you shall not have life in you"

(*John* 6:54)

Catholicism is not a religious sect. It is not a cultural system. Catholicism is not a political program; neither is it a social theory. Catholicism is not even a body of truths to be believed or of precepts to be obeyed. Catholicism is a form of life; it is a life to be lived.

What life, or rather whose life is Catholicism? It is the life of Our Lord and Savior, Jesus Christ. It is the life which He came down from heaven to communicate to men. "I am the way, the truth, and the life." "In Him was life and the life was the light of men." "If any man believe in Me, even though he be dead, he shall live."

Christ came to bring life, a new and undying life, different from and superior to the mere animal life of the body. That life is identified with the divine life by which He Himself lived. Catholicism is that life in the most perfect form under which men can share it!

† Sermon delivered at the holy hour held at Braves Field, Boston, under the auspices of the Archdiocesan Union of Holy Name Societies, June 9, 1946.

Catholicism communicates the life of Jesus Christ through the adorable Sacrament about which the members of our Holy Name Societies are this day gathered. The Blessed Sacrament is the greatest means of perpetuating His life among us that Jesus Christ gave to His Church. That Sacrament is the firm foundation on which rests all else of the faith that we hold. His real presence in that Sacrament is the soul, the sustaining strength, the abiding pledge of our hope here and hereafter. The Eucharistic Bread by which we are nourished—we Catholics of every land and tribe and time—is the undying fountain-head of the charity by which, despite all natural differences, we are supernaturally one. Our faith, our hope, and our charity, all these common bonds by which we are made one with God and united with one another, are vitalized and given their substance by this Bread of Life, *panis vivus et vitalis;* the Bread that is itself alive with God and itself gives life to men!

Catholicism is a form of life. Its life is the life of God, brought down from heaven through Jesus Christ, communicated to us through the Sacrament adored thus publicly here on this altar! For those who accept literally the pledge of Christ there is no other means of access to the divine life. He himself said it: "Except you eat the flesh of the Son of Man and drink His blood, you shall not have life in you!"

To live is to act, and all life manifests itself through its characteristic activity. So the divine life, truly present in the Blessed Sacrament, must reveal itself through the actions of those who are nourished by this Living Bread. Our Catholic faith, centered in this Sacrament, is not merely a speculative system. Our hope, grounded on this Sacrament, is not an ethereal, dream-like ideal. Our charity, vitalized by this Sacrament, is not a remote, pale, mystical sentiment. Faith is not for us a theory; hope is not a deluding opiate; charity is not for us a form of poesy. For men made living members of Jesus Christ by their common Catholicism, for men nourished by the Bread of angels, faith, hope and charity are fountainheads of life, sources of divine action. It is by the active manifestation of these God-centered virtues, not by their mere profession, that we proclaim ourselves to be practicing Catholics.

Faith without works is dead; we must believe unto action, if we would keep our faith alive! The faith must never become something we merely study, debate and defend with argument; it must be something we live. If our faith be a living faith, it will transform everything and everyone that comes within its influence; it will transform and renew the face of the earth! Above all, it will transform ourselves.

Let me recall to you what this living faith unto action did for the ancients. Saint Paul describes its tremendous power to transform when he says: "By faith Henoch was translated, that he should not see death . . . By faith Noe, having received an answer concerning those things which as yet were not seen, moved with fear, framed the ark for the saving of his house . . . By faith he that is called Abraham obeyed to go out into a place which he was to receive for an inheritance; and he went out, not knowing whither he went. By faith he abode in the land, dwelling in cottages with Isaac and Jacob, the co-heirs of the same promise. For he looked for a city that hath foundations; whose builder and maker is God. By faith Sara also herself, being barren, received strength to conceive seed, even past the time of age; because she believed that he was faithful who had promised. By faith Abraham, when he was tried, offered Isaac: and he that had received the promises, offered up his only begotten son . . . By faith also of things to come Isaac blessed Jacob and Esau. By faith Jacob dying blessed each of the sons of Joseph . . . By faith Joseph, when he was dying, made mention of the going out of the children of Israel . . . By faith Moses, when he was born, was hid three months by his parents . . . By faith Moses, when he was grown up, denied himself to be the son of Pharaoh's daughter . . . By faith he left Egypt . . . By faith he celebrated the Pasch and the shedding of the blood . . . By faith they passed through the Red Sea, as by dry land . . . By faith the walls of Jericho fell down . . . By faith Rahab the harlot perished not with the unbelievers . . . And what shall I say? For the time would fail me to tell of Gedeon, Barac, Samson, Jephthe, David, Samuel and the prophets, who by faith conquered kingdoms, wrought justice, obtained promises, stopped the mouths of lions, quenched the violence of fire, escaped the edge of the sword, recovered strength through weakness, became valiant in battle, put to flight the armies of foreigners: women received their dead raised to life again. Others were racked, not accepting deliverance, that they might find a better resurrection. And others had trial of mockeries and stripes, moreover also of bands and prisons. They were stoned, they were cut asunder, they were tempted, they were put to death by the sword, they wandered about in sheepskins, in goatskins, being in want, distressed, afflicted. The world was not worthy of them, though they wandered in deserts, in mountains, and in the dens and the caves of the earth . . . Therefore God is not ashamed to be called their God; for He hath prepared for them a city." (Hebrews 11:5–16).

Such among the Hebrews of old, even before Christ, was the transforming power of faith in Him and in His promises. And, oh, what a creative force faith has been in Christian times! The glorious lives of our own forefathers, who brought their faith to these shores, bear witness to it.

Faith unto action in our own day will generate in us the indomitable spirit of that valiant Catholic bishop who, at the height of red persecution in Mexico, stirred his people with these challenging words: "If one school is closed, open another; if a schoolhouse is torn down, build another; if, in your poverty, you are not able to build, set up tents . . . but fail not in your duty to provide civil and religious education for your children, even if the shade of the trees is the only shelter you can find for your schools . . . If we do but this, the chastisement of the Lord will cease, the awful tempest now breaking upon us will be calmed down and, at last, we shall see in the horizon the light of a new day in which all persecuted men, united by the bonds of a common faith and of a common love, will raise their voices to our Father in Heaven, singing a canticle of praise and of eternal thanksgiving as did the Christians of old when, for the first time, they emerged from the catacombs and were allowed to view again the sun of liberty." Such purposeful faith is the first condition of Catholic life!

Hope, too, must be for us a spur to action; it will be such if it be a hope nurtured by the Blessed Sacrament. The Eucharist is the seed of eternal life; it differs from every form of natural sustenance in that essential respect. It is the reason why we do not fear death; it is the source of the confidence we have that we who are born again of Christ shall be saved forever by hope in Him. He Himself has said it: "I am the bread of life. Your fathers did eat manna in the desert, and are dead. This is the bread which cometh down from heaven; that if any man eat of it, he may not die. I am the living bread which came down from heaven. If any man eat of this bread he shall live forever; and the bread that I will give is my flesh, for the life of the world."

Note well, however, that our hope must also be operative; it must be a spur to action. The Bread of Heaven is not given us for our solace, but that we may live by it; it is not given us for our delectation, but that through us it may be the life of the world. So those who have the living hope that comes from the life that is Catholicism will neither rest in achievement nor despair in defeat; we shall dare all things in the Christ Who is our life. So conquering will be our hope in Him, that no adverse fate we suffer by His permissive Will can possibly overcome it; although He should kill me, still shall I trust in Him.

Charity, third and greatest of the principles of life by which Catholicism and its Eucharistic heart vivifies us in God, must also be for us a spur to action. When the saints, the great masters of the Catholic life, speak to us of charity, of the love that is the life of God, they never do so in terms of repose or of quiescence. They speak of charity as a flame, as a torrential stream sweeping all before it, as a holocaust, as a restless, striving, burning impulse toward God. Charity, most God-like of the virtues, is the most dynamic principle of the Catholic life. God is charity; and he that abideth in charity abideth in God, and God in him. So the life that is Catholicism will manifest itself most perfectly in a proved love for God. The proof of that love is provided by Christ Himself: "If you love Me, keep My commandments." "A new commandment I give unto you: that you love one another as I have loved you." Christ loved us unto the complete emptying of Himself, almost unto His utter annihilation.

He has Himself specified the practical ways in which we may manifest the vitality of our love for Him. These ways are bound up with the spiritual and the corporal works of mercy. You know them well; every Catholic child can repeat them from his catechism. God knows that the times in which we live afford ample opportunity to practice these works of mercy, abundant challenge to the divine life in us which should find expression through them.

The spiritual works of mercy, you recall, are to counsel the doubtful; to instruct the ignorant; to convert the sinner; to comfort the sorrowful; to forgive injuries; to bear wrongs patiently; to pray for the living and the dead. The corporal works of mercy are to feed the hungry; to give drink to the thirsty; to clothe the naked; to harbor the harborless; to visit the sick; to visit the imprisoned; to bury the dead. And the times provide dramatic opportunities to meet the infallible test of our true Christian life as Christ Himself intended the reality of that life should be tested. Catholic Americans, all God-fearing people of the victorious nations, must meditate the challenge to them of Christ's unqualified words: "But I say to you, love your enemies, do good to them that hate you: and pray for them that persecute and calumniate you. That you may be the children of your Father who is in heaven."

I have spoken to you this afternoon of the nature, the sources and the core of the life that is Catholicism. In the natural order men speak of certain signs of life. Before we leave the sacramental presence of Jesus Christ this afternoon, let me suggest to you some of the signs by which men may tell whether we are truly living Catholic lives, whether our faith, hope and charity are really alive, truly spurs to divine activity.

Frequently I receive letters critical of the Church, of its works, of its leaders, of its policies. Some of those who write include the assurance that they do so because they are zealous for its life. Ordinarily, one would not doubt them, and if the reason for their disturbance be what they say it is, then one can welcome the expression of their solicitude. But one has a right to ask greater signs of life than the mere dissatisfaction or even dismay on the part of those who profess to love the Church. To what Catholic organizations do they belong? With what Catholic charitable works are they identified? To what Catholic thoughts have they given expression in their political, social, economic, and cultural activities? Who are their Catholic friends? How Catholic are their homes? How are they received by others who love the Church and are solicitous for its life? We can receive with patience the criticisms of discontented Catholics, but we would receive with joy their co-operation in building up the greater vitality of the Church's life!

We all encounter in our reading, or as we go about to public conferences, the Catholic who protests that his love for the Church and his desire that its life may be lived in the world are the reasons why he opposes so militantly communism, fascism, or some other way of life. One can readily understand why those who love Christ are sometimes preoccupied by the menace of a fascism which would enslave Him or a communism which would murder Him. But opposition to these systems is not itself a proof that one is necessarily anxious to live the Catholic life; a far more impressive sign of life would be a self-sacrificing zeal to present the positive case for Catholicism, a willingness to help educate young men and women so that they may be good Catholics; an anxiety to aid the work of the missionaries who will go to the ends of the earth not to fight a system but to establish Catholicism; I can give approval, for what it is worth, to Catholics who are lecturing on and investigating into the menace of fascism here and abroad; but my approval will be a thousand times more hearty when I see them at prayer with their fellow Catholics and receiving the sacraments and encouraging others to do so, in order that there may be released into society the supernatural energies which will shatter fascism, nationalism or racism. I can give my approval, again for what it is worth, to Catholics who are organizing to stop communism, or who are busily putting others on their guard against its wiles and its wickedness; but my approval will be immeasurably more cordial and infinitely more confident when these same Catholics reveal a practical desire to work with one another in building up the kingdom of God for its own sake, without reference to the safeguards which its moral teaching may give to any past, present or future social system.

More than ever I am convinced that the time has come to consecrate our best energies to thinking out and presenting to others the case for ourselves! We are dissipating our energies, wasting our Catholic life, refuting sixteenth century heresies in the twentieth century, oriental communism in occidental Christendom, the decadent fascism of the Old World in this New World which is too youthful to have any need for reactionary political systems. Militant opposition to these non-Catholic, religious and political heresies may be a mere defense mechanism; it is not necessarily a sign of supernatural life!

Catholicism is a form of life; live it! Grow in it. Become strong with it. Reflect your living faith by positive, constructive works. Confirm your living hope by joyful perseverance through whatever tribulations the living of a Catholic life may entail. Render immortal your lively charity by identifying it, in its source and in its object, with that Eternal God who is your beginning, your end, and all your life.

The Rosary and Catholic Action †

There are three influences in the world today which appear to bring about the downward trend of society, and the rosary is the solution of them all. These three influences are: a distaste for a simple life of work; a repugnance to suffering of any kind; and forgetfulness of the future life.

As for the first, a distaste for the simple life: society is threatened with a serious danger in the growing contempt of those homely duties and virtues which make up the beauty of humble living. We can see it in the home, in the eagerness of children to free themselves from the natural obligation of obedience to their parents, and their impatience to any kind of treatment that is not indulgent and soft.

In the working man this contempt of the old-fashioned but fundamental virtues shows itself in a tendency to desert his trade, to shy away from labor, to become discontented with his lot, to fix his gaze on things that are beyond his reach, and to expect a sudden redistribution of wealth.

The rosary is the answer to all this. If the joyful mysteries of the rosary are impressed upon the minds

† Excerpts from an address delivered at a congress of the Confraternity of Christian Doctrine at New Bedford, Mass., October, 1954.

of people, an object lesson will be given them of the chief virtues that they should practice.

These joyful mysteries remind us of the mysteries and the scenes pertaining to the birth of our divine Lord and His home in Nazareth. Meditating on them we begin to look upon our work not as something lowly and annoying but rather as something desirable and delightful, something cloaked with a certain joyfulness that comes from doing one's duty conscientiously. As a result, home life will be loved and valued highly. And the relations of every man with his neighbor will be blessed by a personal and general atmosphere of respect and charity. If this betterment should go forth from the individual to the family and to communities and thence to the masses in general so that the whole of human life would be lifted to the higher level, who is there who cannot see the lasting good that would be achieved for society?

A second evil responsible for the downward trend of society lies in repugnance to suffering and in eagerness to escape whatever is hard or painful to endure. In this matter, example is everything. And a powerful example of courage will be found in the holy rosary if from our earliest years our minds have been trained to dwell upon the sorrowful mysteries of our Lord's life and to absorb their meaning by calm and silent meditation. In these sorrowful mysteries of the beads we can learn how our blessed Lord began to do and to teach, in order that we might see, written in His example, all the lessons that He Himself taught us by carrying the cross of suffering and sorrow, in order that we might observe how the sufferings which were hardest to bear were those which He embraced with the greatest measure of generosity and good will.

We behold Him overwhelmed with sadness so that drops of blood flow like sweat from His veins.

We see Him bound like a criminal, subjected to the judgment of the depraved, loaded with insults, covered with shame, falsely accused, torn with scourges, crowned with thorns, nailed to the cross, deemed unworthy to live and condemned by the voice of the mob as being deserving of death.

The third evil degrading modern society for which a remedy is needed, is one which is chiefly characteristic of the times in which we live: worldliness. Men in former ages, although they loved the world and loved it far too well, did not usually aggravate their sinful attachment to the things of this world by a contempt of the things of heaven. Even the right-thinking portion of the pagan world recognized that this life was not a lasting dwelling nor our destination, but only a station in the journey.

But men of today, although they have had the advantage of Christian instruction, pursue the false goods of this world in such a manner that the thought of their true fatherland of enduring happiness is not only set aside but banished and entirely erased from their memory, notwithstanding the warning of Sacred Scripture, "We have not here a lasting city, but we seek one that is to come."

From this evil we will be happily rescued by meditating on the glorious mysteries of the rosary. From these mysteries we learn that death is not the end of all things, but merely a migration and passage from life to life. By them we are taught that the path to heaven lies open to all men, and as we behold Christ ascending to heaven, we recall the consoling words of His promise: "I go to prepare a place for you."

Through meditation of the mysteries of the rosary —joyful, sorrowful, and glorious—and through the application of this meditation to our daily works— we can counteract and conquer the greatest influences that tend to degrade society: a distaste for a simple life of work, a repugnance to suffering, and a forgetfulness of the future life. This threefold purpose of the rosary, my dearly beloved friends of Catholic Action, is our greatest prayerful contribution to Christ and His Church in modern times.

Retreat Houses—Schools of Idealism and Self-Denial †

I count this occasion as a most important one in the spiritual history of the Province, so important as to deserve the encouragement and patronage of the most busy of us.

For a full quarter century devout laymen by the thousands, working hand in hand, and, as we might say, heart in heart with the Passionist Fathers, have been building up steadily a tremendous reservoir of spiritual energy in this region by means of the laymen's retreat movement. The Laymen's Retreat House, dreamed by the Passionist Fathers, blessed by the late Bishop O'Leary, made possible by the laymen themselves, has been the powerhouse of this energy.

It is impossible to reckon the good accomplished by the retreat movement, operating within and around your retreat house and sparked by so many of those present here tonight. Only God can tell the thousands, nay tens of thousands of individual lives it has sanctified; the thousands of homes it has strengthened; the countless crises, spiritual or other,

† Address delivered on the occasion of the silver jubilee of the Springfield Laymen's Retreat League at Springfield, Mass., September, 1950.

it has resolved; the wisdom, grace and goodness it has brought to Church and State, to the scores of parishes and civil communities from which our laymen have come to the retreat house and to which they have returned with inspiration and re-birth found here.

The purposes and effects of the retreat movement are many. So far as the Church is concerned, it works wonders by training a spiritual elite among the laity. Retreat houses are, as it were, lay seminaries, cloisters wherein our laymen walk apart with God from time to time in order that they may better serve Him in His Church when they return to their normal pursuits.

The civil society, the local or national community, is mightily served by the laymen's retreat movement. Catholic retreat houses are citadels wherein are inculcated those virtues of loyalty, valor and manly obedience by which the great society is made strong and kept free. Our retreat houses harbor no fifth columnists, no fellow-travellers, no disloyal citizens nor potential traitors. America and the human society may well account retreat houses among their principal assets and the men who frequent them among the champions of our fairest hopes for civic survival and continued freedom.

What does the retreat movement do to the men themselves? What advantage accrues to the life of each of you individually from your association with this movement? What dividend of personal profit does participation in retreat work pay?

The answer might be manifold. For some the retreat movement proves a means to redemption. Every priest and many laymen can repeat stories of souls converted from sin to sanctity, from indifference to fervor, from lukewarmness to zeal as a result of lay retreats. For others the retreat movement proves a means of enormously increasing the good life, adding immeasurably to its consolations and its inward richness. Many of you here present can bear witness to the precious treasures of spiritual happiness and personal satisfaction which retreats have brought into your individual lives. For yet others the retreat movement has been a source of balm and of solace under the buffetings of fate. I well remember what secret strength retreats brought into the lives of service men during the recent war and what consolations retreats have been to bereaved, defeated or disillusioned laymen during periods of economic or political or family crisis.

But to all without exception the retreat movement is at all times a school of supernatural learning, a means of sharpening our vision of the eternal, of deepening our understanding of the divine, of heightening our power to perceive the things which are of God: the truths of faith and the values of the spirit.

These are always the chief accomplishments of the retreat movement. They constitute in a most special way its principal purpose at the moment.

It is a commonplace for preachers to lament the indifference of the age to spiritual realities and to bewail the preoccupation of the day with the purely physical, the strictly material, the carnal and even the obscene. The fact that a truth is commonly stated and constantly repeated may weary us, but it does not make the truth any less true or any more pleasant. The fact is that ours is an age which is spiritually paralyzed by its obsession with the things of sense and by its absorption in the interests of self. Ours is a day which badly needs the unworldliness and self-oblation which are the correctives of these evils, correctives principally provided and most effectively applied in the retreat houses of the laymen's retreat movement.

Unworldliness and self-oblation—these are phrases almost without meaning in our society. In the great struggle to exist, a struggle that in a generation of abortion and race suicide and inadequate housing seems to begin even before birth—self-oblation is a meaningless ideal. In our economic society, with its unbridled competition and aggressiveness, its law of the survival of the slickest; where a man seems able to rise only by tramping down others; where all is one great competition and push for place—the unworldliness of Christ is diametrically opposed to the methods and the maxims of life.

We are living in a fool's paradise about the Christianity of our society. To the extent that our society is secular, it is frankly and shamelessly without religion. To the extent that it denies supernatural sanctions and eternal values, even the occasional phrases in which it seems to speak as would a Christian society, are mere formalities.

Our generation talks of the sovereignty of God—but the notion it has concerning God makes that sovereignty a myth, save to the extent that it is identified with man's own preferences and will. We hear talk of the sanctity of law, but the law for our society, far from being sacred, is more often than not a mere convention agreed upon or arrived at by a count of hands. There is talk of the dignity of the person, but the phrase is almost without meaning since by the person our society usually means only an economic, political, or purely biological unit. Almost none of those who talk nowadays of God's sovereignty, of the law's sanctity or of the dignity of the person means these things literally; they are talking in symbols and they have well-nigh forgotten the meaning of their own phrases.

Even when they keep the letter of the Christian tradition, most of the spokesmen of our secular society totally repudiate its spirit. That spirit is the spirit of Christ, and those who, like yourselves, are banded to increase it by meditation and prayer in retreats must be prepared for a lifelong and a bitter battle to preserve that spirit.

Here in America we profess to have been appalled by the indignities inflicted on the human person throughout Asia and Europe; we say we have been sickened by the desecration of the human body and the disregard of the human soul in the lands of the new paganism. But protests and indignation are not enough. We must re-assert and re-apply the positive Christian understanding of the dignity of the soul and the nobility of the body; we must assert these and apply these in terms of the spiritual philosophy of nature as well as super-nature which it is the business of every retreat to recall and refresh.

When the Catholic Church speaks of the dignity of the person and the beauty of the body it means a dignity and a beauty which are not forfeited either by disease or by death itself. That is the point—or at least the practical point—of the doctrine of the Catholic Church with regard to the bodily Assumption of the Blessed Virgin Mary. This doctrine seems to be on the way to definition as a dogma of the Faith. It should be profoundly understood by members of a spiritual movement like that of the laymen's retreat group.

While I was in Rome this summer there was enthusiastic talk of the announcement that His Holiness plans to proclaim on the Feast of All Saints, November 1, the dogma of the Assumption of the Blessed Virgin Mary. This proclamation, crowning the religious fervor of the Holy Year, will formally define as a doctrine of faith, to be believed and held by every Catholic, that "after her death, the body of the Blessed Virgin, reunited with her soul, was miraculously taken up into heaven."

The definition of the Assumption adds no new element to the Catholic creed, but proclaims in a most solemn form, as an article of faith, what has been the constant Catholic belief and devotion. This belief is commemorated throughout the world on August 15, a holy day of obligation in many countries, as it is here in our own United States.

What is the special significance of this dogmatic

definition for our times? What impetus does it give to the idealism taught in the retreat movement?

Against the background of what I have said tonight about the need of an unworldly and self-sacrificing idealism, the dogmatic definition of our Lady's Assumption has rich meaning. Such a definition at the moment is a magnificent affirmation of the Church's social, as well as theological, creed. No Catholic dogma is "mere theology" in the sense of being without relation to practical realities and to everyday life. Every dogma, properly understood, illumines not merely our faith but our action as well. The Catholic creed does not merely delight our intellects, it colors our values and profoundly affects our practical philosophy. In a world where the human body, despite its pagan cult among the sensual, is held so cheap; at a time when newsreels and current event pictures have revealed human bodies piled like cord wood in camps of horror, or herded, still alive, like the bodies of animals in mobs sent forth to die—in such an age the definition of the dogma of the translation of the Blessed Virgin's incorrupt human body to heaven is a supernatural rebuke to the natural depravity of the times.

There is another lesson for you and me in this dogma as we leave our retreats to go about our daily lives. The incorrupt body which Christian art depicts as mounting to heaven, risen again from death to glory, was the body of a human, a body subject like our own bodies to weakness and weariness, to hunger and thirst, to ache and pain. Under the hot skies of Galilee, Mary knew the harshness of poverty, the dullness of toil. Her action at the Cana wedding feast shows that she was aware both of her Son's power to turn neediness into plenty and of the embarrassments of shortages. Her feet were often bruised on stony tracks, and her tongue was often parched because the longed-for "torrent by the way" was not there. The gospel tells us that our Lord suffered fatigue, pain and physical strain; certainly Mary, a human like ourselves, knew well the afflictions which weary our bodies.

Here, then, is a practical lesson from the dogma of the Assumption. If God, almighty and all-loving, did not spare the body of Mary from privation and suffering, who are we that we should rebel when we, too, are called upon to forfeit some part of our bodily ease? Today most of us have come to believe that our bodies have the right to be pampered. They must be bathed in abundant water, neither too hot nor too cold; they must be clothed from head to foot in garments nicely adjusted to all the dictates of fashion. They must be not only nourished but surfeited with rich food and drink every four or five hours of our waking lives; they must be catered to between meals with confections—stimulants or tobacco; they must be freed from even passing pains by costly drugs; and they must be kept fit by sports and exercise which require special clothes and expensive apparatus.

Not thus fared the body of Mary. She was our Lady of the stable at Bethlehem. She was our Lady of the Nazareth carpenter's shop. She was our Lady of the flight into Egypt. And this is a thought which we may soon need in order to help us through real crises.

After evading it for years, our nation is now having to face the sour fact that the years of destruction, which began in 1939, have left the world poorer, and that, as the President has pointed out within the week, we can only make both ends meet by harder work and plainer living. Spending our capital and juggling with finance have enabled us to cheat ourselves thus far with the delusion that all we have to do is to insist on having anything we want and it will eventually be ours. We are about to be rudely awakened from that dream!

Frugality and austerity are now both our duty and our fate. To be clothed in purple and fine linen and to fare sumptuously every day was a poor ideal yesterday; tomorrow it will have the further disadvantage of being impossible. It will be easier to adjust ourselves to this new order if we cultivate the ideals of unworldliness and self-oblation which are the philosophy preached in our retreat houses, and if we absorb the practical point of the doctrine of our Lady's Assumption: the point of the true dignity, the proper sanctity and the divine discipline of the human body. No real Catholic will ever fall victim to the perverse cult of the body; every Catholic will reverence and serve the proper needs of the body who remembers that God Himself has glorified in heaven the human bodies of the poor Christ and His pure Mother.

However many and depressing the present trials and future discomforts of our national life may be, we can always be sure that the frail hands of God's chosen Mother have been stained and roughened by still lowlier tasks. The Mystical Rose bloomed amidst the thorns of poverty. The Tower of Ivory and House of Gold adorned a wilderness of sharp stones and rude nettles. The Morning Star beamed from a storm-rent sky. The Gate of Heaven crowned a way of sorrows. Even in death, the body of Mary was lovely to God and called out for resurrection and reunion with her soul in the glory of heaven—because she was pure, because she was temperate, because she was austere, because she was disciplined.

I welcome this opportunity to remind those present here tonight, to tell those who hear my voice by radio, that it is precisely to produce persons who will one day deserve resurrection in glory that the Catholic retreat movement exists. Your retreat house has worked to give the Church and America young men and old who are pure; who are temperate; who accept austerities cheerfully; who are willing to lead disciplined lives out of fear of God and love for Christ.

For these past years of work so important for God and country, the retreat house deserves the praise and thanks of men. For like work in the years ahead it deserves the blessing of all who love God, who serve the Church, who fear for America.

With all my heart I proclaim that praise and gratitude—and I beg that blessing. God prosper your work. God keep you all!

Intellectual Honesty: The Great Need of The Hour †

The times are such as call for conciseness, clarity and sure conviction in our thought. They call for courage in the expression of that thought, for courageous conviction in all that we say and in all that we do.

Accordingly, you have chosen well in taking "Courageous Catholicism" as the theme of these deliberations. Your great patron, the renowned convert, John Henry Cardinal Newman, is an exemplar of firmness in the acceptance of the faith, courage in its profession, clarity in its expression.

I give him to you this evening as a model of "intellectual honesty," a virtue which supremely becomes Catholic collegians and for the development of which among you we earnestly pray who seek your well-being and that of Christendom. "Intellectual honesty," in my opinion, was the hallmark of your patron's character; it is the virtue most befitting yourselves.

John Cardinal Newman was an intellectual. He believed in and cultivated "intellectual excellence." He was at home with the things that delight the intellect, that stimulate thought and refresh the mind.

† Address delivered at the Newman Club convention at Wentworth-by-the-Sea, New Hampshire, September 8, 1951.

But he did not make the mistake of supposing that "intellectual honesty" is necessarily the characteristic of all intellectuals, or that intellectual refinement is interchangeable with intellectual honesty.

There were many, even among the great Cardinal's detractors, who were intellectuals even as was he. I suppose that Charles Kingsley, who accused Newman of defending lying and whom Newman proved to be himself a liar, must be accounted an intellectual; certainly he aspired after intellectual excellence and he was at home among the things which delight the intellect, even as was Newman. But in his celebrated controversy with the convert priest, Kingsley revealed himself as lacking in intellectual honesty, though possessed of adroit and slippery, but great, intellectual powers.

What are we to understand by "intellectual honesty"? Well, I always seek to get back to the dictionary definitions of things.

Someone once said that the four gospels, the constitution of the United States and a good dictionary, all three well-thumbed, would be sufficient books to keep the United States free and strong. What does the dictionary tell us about "intellectual honesty"? Webster's guide to the meaning of words declares that "intellectual" as an adjective means "belonging or relating to, or performed by, the intellect . . . things pertaining to the intellect, the mind."

Much more basic to our discussion is the dictionary definition of "honesty." The same Webster tells us that honesty is interchangeable with integrity, truthfulness, freedom from fraud. It explains that honesty implies the refusal to lie, steal or deceive in any way. It includes the concept of integrity, which means such rectitude that one is incapable of being false to a trust, a responsibility or a pledge.

This is very interesting stuff at the moment and well worth our reflection. It could not possibly be more topical. Nothing could be more timely than the evocation of this quality and the meditation of its dictionary definition.

What then is "intellectual honesty"? It doesn't refer to ability in things that pertain to the intellect. Neither does it refer to agility in the use of the intellect. It has nothing to do with I.Q. or any other measure of intellectual power as such.

One may have a tremendous I.Q. and be totally lacking in "intellectual honesty." One may have a relatively great I.Q. and be for that selfsame reason a menace to society itself. Recent history in our own country abundantly confirms these facts.

On the other hand, one may have a very modest I.Q. and have achieved but limited intellectual attainments—and yet be conspicuous for "intellectual honesty," for integrity, freedom from fraud, rectitude in the things that pertain to the intellect; for such rectitude in the use of mental power, such probity in following or accepting the dictates of sound judgment that he is incapable of proving false to a trust, a responsibility or a pledge.

Such is the dictionary concept of "intellectual honesty." The philosopher or the moralist may pursue a little further some of its implications, but the dictionary definition is clear enough for our present purposes. "Intellectual honesty" involves moral considerations. It does not refer to mere mental power, but to the use of that power. It is not limited to the notion of mere ability to think, to judge, to know; it includes an evaluation of the practical consequences and the ideal uses of such ability.

There is no great shortage of intellect in America, in the rest of the world, in human society. In all probability, there is as much intellect at work in the world as there ever was; quite probably there is even more than there used to be. Surely in a world where literacy has become a test of worth and where compulsory education is the established order of things, there must be much more training of the intellect than there was in generations of untutored simplicity and unschooled millions. The power to think, to judge and to know has not been altered in any essential respect within the recorded span of human history. We do not suffer from any dearth of intellect or lack of intellectual power.

Quite the contrary: mere intellect is at times a drug on the market. It has remained for our generation to boast of "Brain Trusts," so superabundant has mere intellect been, just as in plentiful days of another kind, men used to talk of a "Beef Trust," a "Cotton Trust" or an "Oil Trust." And as for trained intellects: were they ever so plentiful as they have become in the last quarter of a century? With the multiplication of methods of testing, requirements for degrees, faculties, courses, institutions, research foundations, laboratories and what not, trained intellects are as plentiful as tabby cats.

But "intellectual honesty" is quite another thing. The righteous use of intellect; the quality of integrity and the acceptance of the conclusions from our own reasonings; probity and rectitude in the use of our very power to reason—who shall say that we have had these in measure overflowing or even sufficient? We have no lack of intellects; but we have an appalling lack of integrity, of "intellectual honesty."

We might put it popularly this way: intellect enables us to know things; "intellectual honesty" impels us to call things by their right names. An intellectual knows, as well as the next man and better than the generality of men, how people become involved in the lives of other people who have made commitments by which they are bound together. But only a man with "intellectual honesty" still labels certain situations "adultery." An intellectual knows why and how budgets appear to balance when in point of fact they do not. But only a man with "intellectual honesty" pins on certain procedures of a political or financial kind the word "theft," and still says "Thou shalt not steal." An intellectual can give us extended explanations of the conflict between loyalties and the trend toward more liberal concepts and revisions of loyalty. But only men with "intellectual honesty" pronounce the word "treason" nowadays when the word "treason" is called for—as the word "treason" has been screamed for, times beyond number, in recent years.

"Intellectual honesty!" If ever as a people we needed one quality more than another, "intellectual honesty" is that needed quality at the moment.

But people say, "The times are so complex! The issues of the hour are so confused! There is such a war of words and conflict of ideas, so much ideological chaos, that all the old simplicities, the homespun virtues are somehow not sufficient. The need is for subtlety, for cunning, astuteness. Simplicity can scarcely stand up to the intricacies of contemporary thought and the complexities of the modern challenge." So runs a familiar plaint.

And it is here that I think of John Henry Newman. Few great men have been possessed of a character so complex. Few, indeed, have encountered problems at once so basic and so bewildering, or have been so repeatedly subjected to attacks from so many sides: from within and without the household of the faith; from at home and abroad, from former friends and present foes; in fact, from inside and outside his own personality.

John Henry Newman presents a character of seemingly completely contradictory powers, virtues and aspects. He was an ascetic, but also an artist and a litterateur. He was a mystic, yet possessed of a shrewd, critically rational streak. He was a lonely man by temperament, yet he had hosts of friends and commanded a tremendous following. He wished no part of the world, yet he displayed an extraordinary gift for perceiving the ways of the world and turning these to advantage. He could be heroic in his renunciation, austere in his forsaking of self and associations and things beloved; yet he was tender to the point of tears. He was cold and ruthless in his reasonings, yet passionate in the impulses of his heart. He would not hurt the feelings of any man if he could help it, and yet he could not help annihilating the prestige of a man whose words or deeds stood in the way of God's truth.

It has been said that we shall never be able to resolve all the paradoxes of Newman's character and mind. He was a maze of contradictions in himself. Moreover, he lived, as I have said, surrounded by conflicts of the most confusing kind. Those upon whom he might logically have relied for encouragement almost invariably walked out on him, opposed him, conspired against him or prescinded from him. Whether in the circumstances of his conversion, or in his controversies, or in his educational work, or in his ecclesiastical career, at Oxford, in Dublin, in Birmingham, in Rome itself, everything seems devious and problematic in its relations to him. Everything is fraught with uncertainties, misgivings, seeming suspicion. Everywhere he encounters contradiction, confusion and challenge.

It is only in the evening of life that Newman could exclaim: "Thank God, the cloud is lifted at last," when Pope Leo XIII gave him the red hat as a recognition of his fidelity at all times to the See of Peter and to the ancient faith.

The life of John Henry Newman, both in its interior aspects and its external relations, was a perpetual quest for light, for certainties. Yet no bewilderment from within nor bludgeoning from without was sufficient to destroy the simplicity with which he perceived things, the straightforwardness with which he expressed his convictions, the rectitude with which he followed up in a practical fashion the conclusions logically reached by the sound judgments of his mind.

John Henry Newman was an intellectual, but he was vastly more than a mere intellectual. He was an exemplar of "intellectual honesty." His intellect, disclosed to him the Church of Christ. His "intellectual honesty" impelled him to enter it, humbly and promptly. His intellect revealed to him both the work that he was called to do in England and the difficulties that would stand in his way; his "intellectual honesty" required of him that he despise the difficulties and give himself entirely to the work, no matter what the toil, the trouble or the outcome.

If he is remembered, as he is, with such admiration after all the years during which so many of his intellectual equals in the Victorian Age have become forgotten—then it is not because of his intellectual gifts, but because of his "intellectual honesty."

You men and women are faced with problems very much like those of Newman's day. Doubt, denial, dissension, violent division: these assail on every side. The old simplicities are scorned; confusion is offered as evidence, forsooth, of richness of thought and abundance of blessing. The call of such an hour is the one that you have made in this convention: the call for "Courageous Catholicism."

It is not enough to be a Catholic at the moment, one must be a heroic Catholic. Catholicism possesses all the truth and vitality in our day that it did in the days of old—but those who profess Catholicism in our day must possess rare courage, courageous Catholicism.

You men and women are blessed with intellects as keen as those of the Victorian Age. One may debate whether the intellect is better trained in our generation than it was then, but the difference is not essential. If you are to serve the Church as Newman did; if you are to be worthy of your name of Newmanites, the name of your collegiate movement, the Newman Clubs; if you are to stand up under the buffetings of the world outside and persevere despite the torment of the world within you: then you must acknowledge that mere intellect is not enough. There is needed something more, a something without which intellect is a power for untold evil, but with which, plus God's grace, intellect can renew the face of the earth.

That "something" is "intellectual honesty," the great need of the hour; the outstanding characteristic of John Henry Newman; the saving moral quality which the dictionary defines in terms of integrity, truthfulness, and freedom from fraud in the things that pertain to the mind.

May God grant this quality to us all. May God help us develop it in ourselves and in our nation. May God restore it to the councils of mankind!

Saint for All †

There is a story told that when Pius IX was pope, a great artist was given the commission to paint a picture to commemorate the proclamation of the dogma of the Immaculate Conception of Our Lady. The scene of the picture was laid in heaven. Pius went to see the sketch of the painting and after considering it a while quietly asked: "And St. Joseph—where is he?" The artist pointed to a group lost in clouds of light and glory and said, "I shall put him here." "No," said the Pope, laying his finger at the side of Our Lord, "but you will put him there, for that is his place in heaven."

In the divine plan of Redemption Mary occupies a unique position as the Immaculate Mother of God Incarnate and no one can approach her in sanctity; but after Mary no one is so great or so privileged as Joseph. His position in the plans of God is immeasurably above all others. By the providence of the Almighty he was chosen to occupy the place of the guardian and protector of the incomparable Virgin Mary and her divine Infant. It was his duty to watch over them, to work for them, and to live in their company.

† Reprinted from *Marist Missions*. (Framingham Center, Mass.), March-April, 1955.

It is a well recognized truth laid down by spiritual writers, that when God selects a creature for any particular position, He confers upon him all the graces and qualifications and perfections that such a position demands. Hence in the case of Joseph we must conclude that he received graces and spiritual favors to an extraordinary degree. How spotless must have been his purity, how ardent his charity, how profound his humility, how consummate his prudence. What exalted sanctity he must have attained and received to be chosen by Almighty God the protector and provider of the home of Jesus and Mary. Yet despite his preeminent holiness and exalted virtues, his whole life is so simple and so ordinary that it admits of imitation by us all.

What, after all, is the essential difference between man today and this glorious saint? The daily worker is tied to laborious, humdrum tasks—so was St. Joseph. If modern man feels at times the weariness of daily toil or the monotony of looking at the same walls and the same faces, so did St. Joseph. Yet he was a great saint. And why? Because in all his actions he had a pure intention, one strong, ruling ambition to love and serve God.

Strange as it may sound, there is no record of even one miracle by St. Joseph performed while living on this earth nor one word he ever wrote or spoke. In silence he followed the instruction of an angel and took a virgin for his spouse; in silence he obeyed the angelic voice and brought her to Egypt; in silence he obeyed another angelic message and brought Mary and her Child back to Nazareth. Poor, lowly, humble, silent Joseph, he did all things well, faithfully, confidently, without questioning that most tender of all wills, the divine will of God.

So, rejoicing, sorrowing, praying and laboring, Joseph passed through life, till at last he fell ill and died, breathing out his pure soul in the arms of Jesus and Mary. His Judge was the One who lovingly clasped his hand as he lay a-dying. The greatest, purest, holiest of all creatures was the one who wiped the sweat from his brow and moistened his parched lips ere he breathed his soul into God's hands. The obscure cave of Bethlehem saw the holiest birth—it was the birth of the Child Jesus. The obscure home of Nazareth saw the happiest death—it was the death of St. Joseph.

To become a saint it is not necessary to change one's daily routine. It is not necessary to be aloof at all times from the conversation and the good cheer of others, to retire into a desert, or to do anything startling or extraordinary. All that is requisite is to avoid and overcome those little faults of daily life, to consecrate one's ordinary daily actions by referring them to God and doing them to please Him and for His sake. In a word, love—love—love God. Be yourself—yes, but see and speak and act with the eyes and the lips and the power of Christ.

If it is too much to expect all to imitate the secret of St. Joseph's sanctity, at least he can be recommended as the advocate of all. St. Teresa of Avila, the saintly and scholarly foundress of the Carmelite reform, has written: "I took St. Joseph for my patron and advocate and I recommended myself increasingly to his protection. I do not remember ever to have asked anything of him that I did not obtain. He assists us in every need."

The modern St. Theresa, popularly called the Little Flower, faithfully imitated the confidence which the glorious foundress of her order placed in St. Joseph. "From my childhood," she writes, "devotion to him has been interwoven with my love for our Blessed Lady. Every day I prayed to him so I felt that I was well protected and quite safe from danger." But notwithstanding these tributes from two of the greatest women of all times, how often do we and Catholics as a whole manifest any special devotion to him?

Poor St. Joseph! With a rare exception here and there, his shrines in our churches are never visited. Seldom is there anybody kneeling before his statue. There seems to be a general conspiracy to keep him as humble as he was in the days when he went about his lowly trade of carpenter. His shrine is erected, he is given the place which the Church insists he shall have ever united with Jesus and Mary, and then he is left alone. How often is there a flower on his altar? How often is there a triduum or a novena in his honor? Not very often. Poor St. Joseph! The greatest saint in heaven, after our Blessed Lady, yet there seems to be little appreciation of his position.

He is the saint for everybody, for sinners, for contemplatives, for priests, for teaching and nursing sisters, for missionaries, for youth, for the married, for the poor, for the workingman, for the dying. There is no age, no sex, no rank, no class, no profession or walk of life whereof he is not the proper patron.

He had a priestly function before priests were ordained, for he was the custodian of the Christ as the ordained are the custodians of the Eucharist. He was the only human confidant of the Blessed Virgin Mary and ever since that time other Marys have been his most faithful clients. Virgins living outside the cloister confidently call on him, for he was the guardian of the Queen of Virgins. Those joined in holy wedlock do well to put themselves under his protection, for he was given supreme charge over the holiest of families. Young men and young women all can find in him a fatherly protector and a wise counsellor who safely guided and tenderly cherished the maiden Mary and the youthful Christ. The rich and the great of this earth can look up to him as the noblest of a royal line. The poor and lowly and those who drain the cup of suffering can best understand him.

Joseph is the saint for all. Patron of the Church, patron of the family, patron of the worker, patron of the interior life, patron of religious and most im portant for the Marists, patron of missionaries.

Our Lady: Queen of Apostles †

The picture conjured up in devout imagination by the title "Queen of the Apostles" is that of the Blessed Mother surrounded by the faithful company of Jesus in the cenacle at the moment of the descent of the Holy Ghost. Together with the apostles themselves, Mary participates in the birth of the infant Church. The Pentecostal fire, which illumines their minds and gives ardor to their speech, somehow communicates itself also to Mary, and to her superabundant graces there are now added new dignities, new privileges and new powers which are apostolic in their nature and effects.

Peter is the prince of the apostles, their visible chief, the vicar of their Christ. But Mary, too, enjoys a primacy all her own. She is the queen of apostles, their heart, the Mother of Christ and, therefore, in a sense, the channel of their apostolic graces as well as the graces of their redemption.

Mary is queen, too, of all others who in any sense share the apostolate of Christ and His Church. That means that she is the queen also of our lay apostles, of those who in every walk of life, within each social class, defend the rights of God, proclaim His truth,

† Reprinted from *The American Ecclesiastical Review,* (Washington, D. C.), April, 1950.

preach His eternal will. As the Queen of these lay apostles, Mary is at once a channel of the grace by which they accomplish their apostolate and an example of the virtues needed in order for them to do so.

Those virtues are *joyous zeal for God and for souls, and a warm love for divine learning*. The lay apostle must have a *will* inflamed with the desire that *God's* will be done and a *mind* steeped in the knowledge of what that will is. Queen of Apostles, Mary is the highest human exemplar of these twin virtues.

The proofs of this are innumerable. The best and the most beautiful is her *Magnificat:* the battle-cry of the true apostle, his paean of praise, his hymn of hope. I offer for your meditation the *Magnificat* and for your imitation Mary of the *Magnificat,* Queen of Lay Apostles.

You and I are used to hearing this glorious canticle in Latin or in English. In both languages it has a magnificent cadence, a majestic, poetic beauty. Let me just repeat for the delight of your ears and the warming of your hearts a few of its stirring lines:

> Magnificat anima mea Dominum. Et exultavit spiritus meus in Deo salutari meo . . .
>
> Quia fecit mihi magna qui potens est: et sanctum nomen ejus . . .
>
> Fecit potentiam in brachio suo: dispersit superbos mente cordis sui . . .
>
> Esurientes implevit bonis, et divites dimisit inanes.

Suscepit Israel puerum suum, recordatus misericordiae suae.
Sicut locutus est ad patres nostros: Abraham, et semini ejus in saecula.

My soul doth magnify the Lord. And my spirit rejoiceth in God my Savior.
Because He hath looked down on the lowliness of His handmaid: for behold henceforth all generations will call me blessed.
Because the Mighty One hath done great things for me: and holy is His name.
And His mercy is from generation to generation: on those who fear Him.
He showeth might in His arm: He scattereth the proud in the conceit of their heart.
He casteth down the mighty from their throne: and exalteth the lowly.
He filleth the hungry with good things: and the rich He sendeth away empty.
He hath received His servant Israel: being mindful of His mercy.
As He spoke to our fathers: to Abraham and to his seed for ever.

Remember, we possess in this great Latin and English poetry not the original, but only translations of translations. Mary uttered her passionate poem of praise in Aramaic. It comes to us translated through Greek, the language of Saint Luke. Saint Luke's

Greek comes to us translated into Latin and from Latin into English. It is easy to appreciate how much of the music and the might of Mary's poem must have been lost in this process of successive translations.

And yet so overwhelming is the thought, so exalted the theme that even in translation four times removed from the original, the words of the *Magnificat* thrill us by their power. They proclaim to us the twin virtues which must characterize the apostle and which are supremely present in the Queen of the Apostles: joyful zeal for God's majesty and for the salvation of souls, a love for sacred learning and divine wisdom.

Joy in the service of God and in the salvation of souls is the recurring theme in the symphony of Mary's *Magnificat, My soul doth magnify*—proclaim the greatness of—*the Lord. My spirit rejoices*—exults in Him. The happiness of what I am doing shall never die. My generation may pass—but *all generations will call me blessed.* The words pour forth unchecked in joy. The song, as always in the heart of the apostle, is one of victory—of visions realized and dreams fulfilled: *for he that is mighty hath done great things for me.*

Joy—joyful zeal—happiness in the doings of God's work: this is the characteristic of the apostle. It is what most we need. It is the great theme of the *Magnificat,* song of the Queen of Apostles.

The object of the apostles' zeal is God's majesty: *holy and terrible is His name.* But it is also the good of souls: that God's mercy may reach them, from generation to generation; that God's bounty may fill them, not let them be sent away empty; that God's justice may rule them in fulfillment of His promise which He gave to our fathers, to Abraham and his seed forever! And out of the apostles' confidence in all this comes one great, sustaining spirit: the spirit of joy, joy in the work, joy in the Lord: *Magnificat.*

These are things of the heart. They are the virtues which strengthen the will of the apostle and feed his zeal to achieve for God. But no less needed are the virtues of the mind, those which store and discipline his intellect.

Mary's Magnificat reveals a mind steeped in the sacred writings of her people—the history, the prophecies, the poetry of Israel, and all in terms of the relation of these to God and of God to them. The phrases of her poem echo the great lines of the Old Testament which record the highest moments of Hebrew history. This great *Te Deum* comes from the abundance of a heart aflame with zeal—but it is also the work of a mind alive with learning and the love for divine wisdom.

Mary prepared for her apostolate by prayer, but also by meditation and study. It was the study of sacred writings which taught her the promises of God to Israel. It was the study of life which taught her all the pathos, the perplexity, the cross-purposes and frustrations of the people, of Israel without the promises.

It was the study of life that gave her an alert and sensitive knowledge of the callousness of the strong, the humility of the weak, the conceit of the "haves," the fears of the "have nots." It was the study of sacred writings which taught her the wealth of examples of God's dealings with men. They knew the story of the Pharaoh of Egypt, Sennacherib of Assyria, Nabuchodonosor of Babylon, Antiochus of Syria—mighty monarchs all, proud ones of the earth whom God had scattered. Esther the humble, preferred to Vashti the proud; her story also Mary had meditated and from it had drawn the rich wisdom of the apostle, who stands before the indifferent and the proud sustained by his knowledge that, even as of old, so now and forever God's victory is certain, final and decisive.

> . . . he scattereth the proud in the conceit of their heart.
> He casteth down the mighty from their throne: and exalteth the lowly.
> He filleth the hungry with good things: and the rich He sendeth away empty.

These are the words of a woman who had prepared for her apostolate by shrewdly watching the ways of the world. She had observed how the subjects of an Eastern king did not approach their sovereign with empty hands: they presented rich gifts to win his favor. In turn the typical Eastern monarch did not allow himself to be outdone in generosity; he bestowed liberal rewards on his favorites. His humbler subjects could not afford costly gifts and so could not "get in." Mary had seen this times beyond number.

But she had also seen that with God it is different—and that knowledge underlies the wisdom which is the secret and the spur of the apostle. To know the ways of the world—but to meet them with better ways, better and wiser and more effective. To understand the ways of men—but to act with the wisdom of God. To apply the lessons learned of life and of study—but apply them God's way: all this is the work of the apostle, and of this work Our Lady is the great exemplar. Her *Magnificat* sings the joy and the wisdom of all apostles, the informed enthusiasm which I pray will be yours.

Queen of Apostles, pray for us. Pray for the Church at whose birth you were present. Pray for the Church of whose apostles you were the companion in perseverance and in prayer. Pray for the Church which is the Mystical Body of that Christ whose physical Body was fashioned of your flesh. Pray for us who hold the place of the apostles in this century, who strive to do their work, who lack so many of their graces but must somehow accomplish a task like to theirs; give us enthusiasm and joy in the knowledge, the love and service of the Lord. Queen of Apostles, pray for us all!

Three

TYPES OF LAY ACTION

Your Purpose in Life †

Everyone, every man, woman and child, requires something to live for. No life has meaning or value until purpose enters it. One of the worst features of times of unemployment and depression is the way the lives of men and women, of boys and girls, so speedily lose point, they seem to have nothing to live for. If, in times of such crisis, some great cause captures their imaginations, some powerful purpose is offered to them, even though it be evil, that purpose may mobilize and master such people.

Something like that is happening every day. Into tens of thousands of lives made empty and pointless by secularism, defeatism, and social chaos, there has entered all the dreadful motive, the evil purpose, the thrilling sense of a part to play and a destiny to fulfill which came with the communist idea.

A young man, a member of Stalin's machine, once explained how he came to be caught up in the frenzy of the communistic drive. "No one had wanted me before," he said; "I had nothing to live for—there was no reason and no place and no purpose for me. Then the communists came. They gave me a purpose

† Excerpts from an address delivered in Boston on the occasion of the seventy-fifth anniversary of the Massachusetts Catholic Order of Foresters, April 4, 1955.

and brought me together with an army of others who had the same purpose. I began to live!"

There is never any excuse for the life of a Catholic being without purpose. There is never any reason why the life of a Catholic should lack meaning. Every Catholic entirely apart from the human interests he may share with others, has something worth living for, something worth dying for, a purpose so powerful that it moved the Eternal God Himself, inspired the incarnate life of His Redeemer Son and gave that life its meaning. For this purpose Christ came into the world: that He might preach in towns and villages, in public places and in secret, the glory of God, the salvation of men, the coming of the Kingdom that would unite God and Man forever. And that purpose, a purpose worthy of the Son of God Himself, Christ gave to the lives of His apostles and disciples, to my life and to yours, to the life of every person baptized in His Name, confirmed in His Spirit, fortified by His sacraments.

We call ourselves Christians. The word should mean that Christ is as much a part of us as we are a part of ourselves. It should mean that self and class and family and nation and every other interest which may move a man's heart hold second place to Christ in our lives—we are renewed in Him. If we are, though the renewal may be on the hidden level of the soul and of sanctifying grace, its effects will be visible to all; the whole world will be able to witness the change Christ makes in us. When the purpose that is Christ's dominates the life of a Christian, everything about him is made different. All that he is and all that he does—all that he is at home, all that he does abroad—all the things and all the persons he knows and loves are affected and made better. They are themselves renewed by the contagious power of Christ at work through the convinced Catholic. The friendships we make, the pleasures we enjoy, the thoughts we think, the things we do and the things we leave undone—all these should take on their purity, their integrity, their value, their purpose from the strict identity between our purposes and the purposes of Christ.

The supremacy of Christ in our purposes will give new meaning both to adversity and to the good things of life. Remembering Christ, we will not be scandalized or discouraged, fearful or ashamed even when religion, when the very things of Christ seem endangered or defeated.

All people who walk with Christ, as you have pledged yourselves to do, will go with Him against wind and tide, in His rags as well as in His silver slippers, yes and stand by Him when bound in irons as well as when He walketh the streets with applause.

If you are a doctor to men, you are called to be a man of God to other doctors. If you are a teacher of children, you are called to be an apostle to other teachers. If you are an engineer, a tradesman, a technician, a laborer in the city of men, you will influence the men of your unions, your syndicates, your professional groups to aid you and to aid Christ in the building of the city of God. If you are a businessman in the marts and market places of the world, you will become the associate of Christ in promoting His

Father's business wherever men of good will are to be found. And if you translate your religious fervor, your loyalty to and your love of Christ into the performance of your duty as a citizen, you will purify politics, government, and the Christian way of life.

God's Will, Our Work †

I have come a long way to be with you, but I want you to know that I come with a sense of personal pleasure and not merely official responsibility.

Quite frankly, despite my post as episcopal moderator of the National Council, I would have hesitated in this particular season to put aside my engagements at home and venture so far from my crowded desk in Boston were I not persuaded of the very great importance of your gathering and of the work to which you are dedicated.

I dare even speak of the supreme importance of that work since, as the theme of our Congress proclaims, it is none other than God's will, the sovereign norm, the overriding consideration of all that is and especially of all that we do.

"God's Will, Our Work." Such is the brief yet all-inclusive statement of the relationship between God's purposes and the programs of those who, believing in Him, seek to do His will. Such is the foundation of the special dignity, the divine importance of the activities of Christians, of Catholic Action in the sense that your Council understands it.

† Address delivered at the twenty-sixth national convention of the National Council of Catholic Women at Seattle, Washington, September 21, 1952.

Our works are not merely performed in humble obedience to God's will; that alone would render them meritorious and admirable. The works of the Christian are far more significant; in a literal sense, they are the means to the accomplishment of God's will. The purpose of God, the building up of His kingdom on earth, the fulfillment of His plan, the accomplishment of His will—all these depend, in greater measure than most appreciate, on whether we do the good works we should, when we should, how we should and as we should.

Sometimes Christians misunderstand the relationship of their works to the unfolding of God's providence. They exaggerate, if the word is not misleading, not so much the omnipotence of God as the relationship of His omnipotence to the plans of His providence. The devout assert accurately enough that without God we can do nothing, but they forget that even with Him, God requires that we do our part if His will is to be brought to pass on earth as it is in heaven. The believing understand that God's will must prevail in the final analysis, whatever the wicked, stupid or even worthy efforts of men—but they sometimes forget that God's will includes the requirement that we work as if everything depended on us even though we must pray as if everything depended on God.

In this sense, then—a sense which no right-thinking Catholic will misunderstand—the accomplishment of God's Will depends on our work even as, though not as much as, the worthiness of our works depends on God. You all know the funny story told a thousand times to illustrate this point. It is the story of Mike, the inevitable hero of all Irish yarns, who found himself without a job and went to his pastor with a proposal. He said to the pastor: "I have a good idea. The parish has all that new property you bought for an eventual school. You can't use it until the depression is over. Meanwhile, it is covered with rubbish and has become an eyesore and a danger. It's useless to you and a nuisance to the neighborhood.

"Why not turn it over to me for a couple of years? I will clean it, plow it, plant it, care for it, improve it and so support myself by turning it into a garden. When the depression ends I'll get a steady job and give the place back to you, improved a hundredfold."

The pastor agreed and so it was done. Mike worked like a Trojan from early spring until the harvest. Then he brought the pastor down to see the wonders he had accomplished. He pointed out the rows of beans where before had been tin cans; the glorious corn where once had been heaps of junk; the attractive flowers in place of the skunk cabbage, poison ivy and ragweed. He was bursting with pride.

The pastor looked it all over and then deflated poor Mike with a single sentence. "Isn't it marvelous," he said piously, "marvelous what God can do?"

"Marvelous what God can do?" shrieked Mike, "say, do you remember this place when God was working it alone?"

Poor Mike was a better theologian than the pastor. It is marvelous what God can do, but it is also wonderful the way that the accomplishment of His will depends on the free, generous, dedicated cooperation of us; in a word, on our work. The world is very much like the lot of land that the pastor loaned to Mike. It has been made ugly by the accumulated debris of old errors, foolish mistakes, pathetic blunders, grave sins. It has been made dangerous by the heaped-up junk of irresponsible ideas, misleading maxims and perilously false principles which have been hatched and let loose through the centuries in our civilization. All this is contrary to God's will, but it will not be corrected except by God's grace plus our work. That is why God's will is our work, why our work must be in accordance with God's will.

God does not intervene miraculously in the direction of history. Rarely indeed do the heavens split and the voice or the hand of God emerge to turn the tides of things or forcibly direct into better ways the fortunes of men or nations. A few times God has spoken from the mountain top or through His prophets; once He spoke unmistakably through His Son and always He teaches through His Church. But almost never, even in these cases, does He achieve His purpose directly and without reference to human cooperation. Normally God works His will through secondary causes, through human agents. That is where we, priests and people in Catholic Action, loom so large in the total picture of God's providence for the world, the accomplishment of His holy will.

It is God's will that the world be peopled with intelligent beings freely contributing to His glory and accomplishing His purpose. And so God committed to our first parents, and to all parents since, the mighty work of co-creation in the words: "Increase and multiply and fill the earth!"

It is God's will that man, made in His image, should achieve dominion over all nature less than human, administering creation in a stewardship answerable to God. And so God made the works of His hands the objects of our work of research, scientific study and patient mastery as little by little we discover through hard work and bend to our purposes and to God's the secrets of the universe.

It is God's will that society be peaceful and orderly, a foreshadowing of the kingdom of God, and so we are commanded to do the works of peace and to strive to accomplish whatever will promote that blessed condition of society.

It is God's will that good triumph over evil, truth over error, faith over confusion, freedom over despotism, and so we are charged by Jesus to be doers of the word, not hearers only, so that society may practically benefit from those teachings of Christ which would otherwise remain abstract principles, theoretical truths, unless God's will becomes our work.

This, says St. Paul, is the will of God: your sanctification. It is God's will that we be saints, but we become such only through the constant doing of the works of justice, charity, mercy and wisdom. It is God's will that we work out our salvation, perfecting ourselves by the works made possible by His grace and directed by His will.

Wherefore, you have chosen well the theme of this great congress:

"God's Will, Our Work."

Let all your deliberations, plans and programs for the months ahead make clear that you yourselves understand the theme you have proclaimed. If someone ask you: "What is God's will for the world?" do not merely answer: "Peace!" Say rather: "It is God's will that we do the things that are necessary in order to bring peace to pass. It is God's will that we study, reason, sacrifice, cooperate, in a word work, so that peace may be assured."

If someone ask you: "What is God's will for America?" do not glibly answer: "Prosperity!" Say rather: "It is God's will that we so struggle, strive, save and even sweat by intelligent work that we may certainly deserve and perhaps achieve national prosperity."

If someone ask you: "What is God's will for our families?" do not easily answer: "Sanctity!" Say rather: "It is God's will that the example of parents, the imitation of children, the lives of families take the form of deeds which are holy, works which are spiritual, so that homes may be blessed and families may be strong!"

If someone ask you: "What is God's will for me?" do not answer: "Salvation!" Such answers leave out too much. Say rather: "It is God's will that I work out my salvation by doing all those things which will render it certain and avoiding whatever works would render it impossible."

"God's Will, Our Work." See how bound up they are with one another, how remote is God's will without our works, how pointless would be our work without God's will.

And so I return to the programs of the National

Council during the months ahead. Place each of them singly and all of them together in the context of God's will. Then you will be able to evaluate them objectively and to support them enthusiastically, as you would support a spoken request of Jesus Christ made directly to you.

Accustom yourselves to think of the work more often in terms of its relationship to God's will, less often in terms of immediate, more superficial considerations. Then when you pray: "Thy kingdom come! Thy will be done, on earth as it is in heaven!" you will be consciously praying not only for the glory of God but for the graces needed to do your own work, for your work and God's will will be intimately identified the one with the other.

Is it God's will that we have sound laws, just institutions, sane traditions? Of course it is. But the immediate will of God is that my works, your works, our works, the works of our councils be consistent with these desired objectives. It is God's will that we work to bring to pass these ideals.

Is it God's will that we have high moral standards among the mature, purity among the young, decency in the general community? Of course it is. But these blessings will not be secured by a miracle. They will be assured only to the extent that singly and in organization we work for the enforcement of existing laws consistent with decency; for the correction of scandal wherever reinforcements, reforms or new directions may be required to achieve God's will in the field of private, family or public morality.

Is it God's will that we have efficient hospitals,

good schools, adequate housing, healthy human relations, friendly exchange within our neighborhood, strength at home and good order abroad? Surely all these things are God's will. But that is only half the picture. These must be the objects of our works as well or they will remain God's will and be without root, branch or flower among us.

The need for these must be the theme of our preaching work in the parishes. The means to these must be the object of our teaching work at home. The techniques for achieving these must be the concern of our study work in our various groups. The hastening of these must be the inspiration of all our organized work on the national level. The perfection of these must be the motive of our cooperative work with others.

"God's Will, Our Work." This is the theme of your convention; let it be the strength of your future endeavor, so that the more you work the more perfectly you will attain in yourself and achieve with others that will of God in which lie our peace, our perfection and our salvation.

I have been telling you how God's will depends, in a sense, on our works if it is to be done on earth as it is in heaven. Let me now suggest the other side of the medal which is that our works depend for their perfection on conformity with God's will.

God wills what is good; He wills not what is evil. It is our duty to will in conformity with Him; to resist what He wills not.

The discovery of the will of God so that our works may conform with it is the chief business of life; it is assuredly the supreme end of all education worthy of the name.

Christians understand that as a matter of course, but so do enlightened pagans. That is essentially what Plato meant when he said that the primary purpose of education is the learning of the distinction between right and wrong.

God wills what is right. He wills not what is wrong.

Unfortunately mere knowledge does not make clear what is right and what is wrong, nor does education of the mind alone provide insight into the distinction between the two. The will of God may be the object of intellectual reflection and study; it reveals itself fully, however, only to those whose own wills, whose hearts, are open to its influence.

Failure to appreciate this integral, all-embracing character of moral education, with the consequent pathetic trust in purely intellectual knowledge, has led us far down the garden path of folly and of evil. It has led to the sad delusion that evil, sin and crime are due to ignorance, and that if we educate by imparting knowledge we will abolish crime.

Spokesman of this fallacy was the patron of non-religious education, Guizot, who boasted: "When we open a school, we close a prison." That was three generations ago—and bitter years between then and now have given him the lie. We have opened ten thousand schools and more since then—but we have closed no prisons.

Never before in the history of the world was there so much accumulated knowledge or so much knowledge so widely dispensed. Yet rarely before has there been so little effective knowledge of God's will, of the distinction between right and wrong.

The proof? As a people we spend more for education than any ten nations; more each year than any ten years of a generation ago. We have endowments for universities, research institutes, fact-finders and science, we have the just less than infinite resources of the tax powers behind our state and municipal schools.

For all that, our crime bill today is $40,000,000 a day. Our prison population has doubled while the general population was rising by one-fifth. We have the largest homicide rate in the world. The rate has doubled in thirty years. In normal times our murder rate is from 6 to 40 times that of European countries. A major crime is committed every 24 seconds. We have a murder every 40 seconds!

In the face of this we can only conclude that the trained intellect is not a complete guide to the knowledge of the will of God, certainly not a sure guide to this most important moral knowledge. We must conclude that it is not the intellects of the world which have broken down; it is the consciences of our generation which have collapsed. It is through the education of conscience that the will of God becomes clear.

That is why your slogan, "God's Will, Our Work," commits you unreservedly to work for whatever is needed to educate consciences. It means that you are for religious schools wherever they are needed and possible. It means that you are for maximum moral education consistent with truth in all educational programs. It means that you are for legislation which permits access to moral education under religious auspices, whether by released time, dismissed time or whatever other technique will meet the needs of conscience.

Thus will you help make known by work that will of God which is the model of your work. Thus will you promote the national welfare which, quite as much as that of the Church, is the object of the work and the prayers of the National Council of Catholic Women.

The Church promotes the national welfare in many intimate ways. We are the Church; I am; you are. Most particularly, we represent the Church when we are banded together in the National Catholic Welfare Conference, of which this Council is an integral part, a principal agency. In this organized capacity we have the high duty to cooperate with the hierarchy in the work of forming Christian conscience both in individuals and in the social group. Thus, as we have seen, we shall be helping clarify the will of God for our generation.

Part of the work of forming Christian consciences requires of the Church that she strive to remove obstacles to virtue in personal and social life. The Church thereby helps the State to preserve internal peace and security.

The field of politics sometimes presents many obstacles to virtue. It is the duty of public officials to promote the common good. If any action of theirs brings injustice or persecution to a minority group or even to one citizen, it is the duty of the enlightened conscience, of the Church, of you and me to oppose such action at once. The Church must also oppose the passage of bills which would hamper the free exercise of religion or contravene the dictates of the moral law. Frequently the Church must urge the passage of laws consistent with sound religion, wholesome morality or public decency.

When the Church thus takes cognizance of pending legislation or executive action you immediately spring into action. Through the National Catholic Welfare Conference, the Church in America is kept aware of legislative and social trends in the country, indeed in the general world community. Through it, and specifically through you, the Church speaks to favor, oppose or suggest legal action or national policies which affect morality and virtue, which apply the practical corollaries of the law of conscience, which bring American life into conformity with God's will so far as the divinely guided Church and the supernaturally enlightened conscience can determine that will.

The heavens do not split in order that God may cry out against graft, special privilege, protected crime or evil political philosophies, all these violations of God's will. It is your work to utter God's cry of protest. No angels descend to trumpet approval from the sky of those things which promote the national welfare because they are in accord with God's will. It is your work to speak up as God would will when there is need of support for virtue, sanity and good order. Sometimes the cry of protest or word of support does not even come from the Church in the sense of the "official" Church; sometimes the cry or word must be yours, individually or in organized Council, as you do the works by which you bring to pass God's will.

See how close to God your Council is. See how your work is His will. See why God wills your work! See why it is with confidence that I beg His blessing on you–and the work.

The Role of Women as Crusaders Against Immorality †

There are two threats which particularly menace our society and which Catholic women of your spiritual idealism almost alone can control. The first is a menace to natural life itself; the second is a menace to the supernatural life of the soul. Both menaces are rampant in our land, and so long as they are, they must constitute the chief objects of your opposition as they are the chief obstacles to your idealism.

The safety of human life is threatened by the militarists on every side, by the red fascist politicians, by the cold and calculating diplomats who impose peace terms and tolerate regimes under which political and ideological interests take precedence over human rights, personal dignity, and the very lives of millions. The safety of human life is menaced by irresponsible military control of atomic energy. The safety of human life is menaced by secret treaties. The safety of human life is menaced by political appeasement of military regimes already on the march toward the conquest of the most ancient nations of Christendom.

If the natural life of the body is threatened in our

† Excerpts from an address delivered at the sixth biennial meeting of the National Catholic Laywomen's Retreat Congress held in Philadelphia, October 12-13, 1946.

secular society, the supernatural life of the soul is in even greater jeopardy. To the extent that they are mortal sins, or involve them, the menaces to the natural life of the body are also threats to the supernatural life of the soul. I must particularly mention, however, one column of attack on the life of the soul which women like yourselves must be prepared to meet with all the spiritual energy at your command. I refer to the output of a considerable section of the "literary" and "artistic" spokesmen of our secular society. Some of this does not pretend to any literary excellence; the cynical, perverse pandering of our "keyhole columnists," for example, and the frankly pornographic slant of the newspaper and billboard advertisements of the cruder plays and motion pictures of the moment. These do not pretend to any excellence. But not a few of the principal moral perverters of our society are ladies and gentlemen who ask to be accepted as authentic leaders in the realms of the intellectual and the cultural.

Christians know that filthy books and degenerate plays are the death of the supernatural life of the soul. And, so, they are prepared to use all the strength of Christian idealism in the battle against these. But there is another angle to this, an angle which suggests to me that the State has also an obligation to put its resources to work against the spread of obscene literature and the production of degenerate plays, if it be found that book publishers and theatre guilds do not intend themselves to clean house and to recognize their responsibility regarding the moral condition of the nation. The general decline of individual morality in our country is due in good part to the "canonization," so to speak, of jungle ethics in our novels and stage plays; this is the principal reason for the cynicism with which persons and nations greet American efforts at moral reform on the international level. At the present moment America is demanding a high standard of political morality of nations all over the world. Together with our allies in the recent military victory, we Americans are sitting in judgment on social malefactors in Europe and in Asia. We are handing down high-sounding verdicts in their regard, and are dealing out severe penalties for the damage they have done and for the many they have killed.

There is something hollow about our moral pretensions, however, and something almost hypocritical about our crusade for international righteousness, so long as America gives such grudging support to the agencies within our own land which are working for individual and family morality.

Many of the writers and artists who specialize in depravity here at home are at the same time specialists in lecturing and protesting about the terrible political world we live in, and are constantly complaining about the lack of morals exhibited by diplomats and by nations. Many of the publishers of immoral books and the producers of immoral plays are among the leaders in the various organized groups which are always trying to lend their influence to solving the world's problems.

These persons do not seem to realize that there can be no decent moral standards in the relations between nations so long as decent moral standards do not prevail among individuals here at home.

It has not occurred to them that, so long as they themselves are accepted by Americans as experts in international morality, it is useless to expect that America will ever be taken seriously by those who hope to solve the problems of the world, or that America can ever convince other nations that peace lies in the application of moral principles and worthwhile ideals.

For the good of our souls and for the good of the world, America must repudiate the international moral pretensions of individuals who here at home pander to every depravity and who contribute, more than any other single group, to the moral decline of our nation. We have protested against and punished the international criminals who kill the body. It is time that we took up the cudgels against the enemies within our own household who seek to kill the soul of our nation and the supernatural lives of our children.

Christian Co-Existence †

Each age has its challenge and in each age Catholic women, witnesses to Christ and lovers of His Mother, must make to that challenge a response which echoes the will of God.

In our own age the challenge is manifold; the answer to it has the simplicity of God Himself and the consistency of His divine revelation.

On the world front the challenge of the day is that of the disunity which plagues mankind. As if in despair of any hope of uniting all the men and nations of the earth in a single cooperative society, we talk now of "co-existence."

The very word suggests our divisions. Far from being the label of a bond among the peoples, "co-existence," even if it were possible, would be the acknowledgment of our agreement to disagree and of our reluctant but real intention to remain apart from one another.

I say "even if it were possible," because it must be obvious that "co-existence," as frequently defended, is an empty and dangerous delusion. The simplest meaning of the word is, by genuinely human standards, without any implication of warmth, love or

† Address delivered at the Congress of the League of Catholic Women in Boston on May 9, 1955.

respect—it states merely the unavoidable fact that the races of mankind exist together here on earth. The vision of co-existence which modern peoples cherish as a sturdy anchor of peace, a vision based on fear, is incapable of realization so long as there prevails the current attitude of dreading war as the greatest of tragedies and, at the same time, of placing all trust and confidence in the instruments of war.

The concept of co-existence which permeates the thinking of so many world leaders today—and which, tragically, has been adopted by thousands of the unthinking in every walk of life—regards peace as a sort of stalemate, the consequence of a balance of material and economic power so exquisitely fine that no one dares upset it lest the first to make a move destroy himself, along with the world. Such co-existence falls far short of facing the challenge of the age. It is not a question of our existing together—that is a fact—but of mankind's alternatives of living together as one family or destroying itself completely!

Armed conflict is one form of destruction. Nuclear weapons are swift and decisive instruments contrasted with which the destruction wrought by past armed conflicts can be reckoned as nothing. No war, however, and none of the weapons of war are potentially so dangerous as the belief that the unity of mankind can ever be achieved by "co-existence" in that state of fear which saps our race of its most cohesive elements, mutual love and respect among nations and men. Such a co-existence, far from achieving peace, bears within it the seeds of further and more devastating conflicts because it has no regard for human dignity, national integrity or the rational and moral principles underlying peace, but looks with blind eyes only to expediency and to the fancied security of military might.

The answer to the challenge of co-existence cannot be found on the drafting boards of modern technologists, nor in the economists' claims, nor in the political maneuverings of statesmen, however well-intentioned these may be, for the peace we seek cannot be guaranteed by the productivity of industry or a balanced budget or the shrewdly practical working of diplomacy. Peace is order, and that order is found among men, not among machines. Christ alone is capable and willing to unite the minds of men in that truth and love that dispel error and fear, making possible mankind's dwelling together as one family under God, rather than by mere co-existence, as in a contest for group survival.

The foundations of human unity, which is the only answer to the problems of our world, are, as the Holy Father has pointed out, neither technical, political nor military. The bridge of peace is built of spiritual and moral fabric and those who stand for peace and unity among men must also stand resolutely for fear of God and His judgment rather than suspicion of neighbor and his intent, must hold for principles of truth, love and justice—as things to be communicated to all phases of human life—rather than for error, expediency and hatred.

The conduct of Christians, therefore, of good women like yourselves throughout the world, whether of high state or low, must be resolute in receiving and finding in divine charity in practice that active assistance towards a *Christian* co-existence, the unity of mankind in the family of Christ, which alone can be efficacious of peace.

In the life of the Church the challenge of our times is that of bringing back to the Church and to the sacraments the faithful who have lapsed from its unifying fold. This second challenge is one of which we, as individual Catholics, are frequently all too unaware. The fact remains, however, that every move to win back for Christ one of His lost sheep is also a move in the direction of achieving that larger unity among mankind that is the solution to the problem of co-existence.

The "one world" of yesterday's dreams has become the two worlds of today's reality. Of these worlds, one stands for Christ and His standard and the other, for the forces of anti-Christ. "Whoever is not with me is against me," Jesus said, and His words are a solemn reminder of our obligation to rally all mankind to His side. What better beginning can we make than to seek out those who once knew Christ—loved Him deeply, perhaps—but who, having for one reason or another forgotten Him, now walk in the darkness of infidelity and of sin.

Love, it is said, diffuses itself. It is like a spark igniting the tinder, bursting into flame, consuming everything within its reach so as to transform what it touches into heat and light. If we really love someone, we desire nothing more than that he should share our happiness. If we really love our neighbor, as God expects us to, it disturbs us greatly to see the emptiness of his life, devoid of the consolations and joys of the religion he once professed and whose imprint he will always bear.

The Catholic laity of our day must never forget that Christ's mandate to the apostles, "Teach ye all nations . . . preaching the gospel to every creature . . ." was addressed not merely to priests and bishops but to them, as well. From the moment of confirmation, every Catholic person has an obligation to bring the truths of Christ to those who do not know Him and to those who, having known Him, have forgotten Him.

You must never adopt the philosophy that the conversion of lapsed members of the flock is none of your concern. It is! Lapsed Catholics are unhappy Catholics, though at times they seem able to lull conscience into a feeling of false security and imagined spiritual peace. Without Christ, without the channels of grace His Church provides, their lives are purposeless and their apparent happiness a sham! Failing our attempt to help them, without our efforts to stir in them again that spark of faith that once kindled in their souls God's love, their road through life is a most tragic one.

Most of us are genuinely convinced that we do have an obligation to spread the faith; but, almost as though we feared the effort, we rarely bother to particularize our conviction with regard to those who have left the Church. We acknowledge that the faith is a source of joy to us. We accept without question that our lives are truly complete only insofar as our faith permeates every aspect of them. But we must also realize that our neighbor, of whom we so often say, "I think he's supposed to be a Catholic" . . . or . . . "Well, she used to go to church," is no less needful of Christ and the Church than we ourselves.

Our mistake has been the failure to make our thinking concrete and practical—to think of the Church's necessity and of the necessity of the faith in the lives of men not merely in a general and abstract way but in terms of living individuals of our acquaintance. We shall never make converts by dreaming of the total, simultaneous conversion of all the people on earth! The Church, faced by the challenge of bringing lapsed Catholics back to Christ and the sacraments, exists here and now. It is not a Church of nameless, unidentifiable masses! It is a Church of individual men and women, of whom many are in the state of God's grace, some are sinners courageously seeking their way back to that grace and some, oblivious of the fact that Christ's crimson blood was shed also for them, have wandered from the fold. The Church includes you and me, but it also embraces my neighbor whose ignorance or malice has caused him to repudiate it. He is just as much a source of concern to me—or so he should be—as the upwards of thirty-million Catholics of our land who are loyal to Christ.

So, the Church exists at this present moment and each of us must choose—by name and individually—those unfortunate brethren in whose lives the light of faith has been dimmed or snuffed out, so that we may undertake the task of extending the kingdom of God to them, causing them to see once more the beauty of Christ's truths, to know again the security of His embrace and the peace of union with the Church. Christ Himself summons us to answer the challenge.

Finally, in our personal lives there is the challenge of our failure faithfully to reflect the image of Christ in us, individually. It is not enough that we think grandly of doing our bit to effect the unity of the human race in Christ. It is vain to feel that we can win back fallen-away brethren merely by praying for them even though they need our prayers and God expects us to pray. The challenges of our age demand that we become apostles who will make the truth visible first of all in our own persons, lovable by the attractiveness of the manner of our lives, and worthy of admiration by becoming ourselves, insofar as is possible, living examples of Christian virtue.

We cannot win people to the side of Christ and of religion merely by arguing with them. Argument oftentimes generates more heat than light, but if you let a person see the thing you are trying to explain he is apt to agree with you and, more important, to do what you wish. The wonderful thing about our Christian faith is that it gives evidence not only of what Christ taught but of His very Person—the way in which He lived! Our faith is not just another creed to which we must give intellectual assent, but something alive in creatures of flesh and blood like you and me. I might be a teacher—the author of a dozen books—and you could follow out my teaching to the letter, yet know nothing at all about me as a person.

Christ not only preached God's word, but in Him "the Word was made flesh."

Men are governed and souls are won not by words alone, but by the reality of things. Had Christ depended on the sound of His voice alone to put across to His hearers the lessons of the Sermon on the Mount, even His effort might have met with failure. People listened to Him and took it to their own hearts when He said that the poor were blessed because they had first seen with their own eyes that He was among the poorest of the poor. It was the example of Christ that strengthened the credibility of His words and gave them life.

The Abbé Perreyve used to pray: "Jesus, when they see me may they recognize Thee." Such should be our prayer, too, if we are to accept the third challenge of our age, that the image of Christ find faithful reflection in our lives. We live amidst people, more of them than we can possibly tell in this country of ours, who know neither Christ, nor His gospel, nor the Pope, nor the bishops, nor the priests of the parishes in which they live. They know only themselves, their neighbors, their neighbors' children, the men and women among whom they work and take their recreation. In other words, they know only people like yourselves—and the surest possibility of their coming to know Christ and the Church is by seeing Christ in you!

Whenever such people see you, wherever you may be, no matter what the circumstances, you and you alone will have the privilege of introducing them, as it were, to Christ. When they see you, it is important that you be the occasion of their learning something, at least, about Catholicism of which they are so woefully ignorant. When you see them, you must be prepared to show them Jesus Christ, because for that once you are Christ—all that they can see of Him, and the Church, all that they can know.

Our Lord once warned us about concealing our light, the light of the living faith within us. He told us that it should be so placed as to cast the warmth of its friendly rays all about. In accordance with the gifts with which God has blessed us, we are obliged to make known Christ's truth by letting it shine forth from our lives, to penetrate our surroundings like leaven in the dough, rather than let ourselves be dragged down to the mediocre level of a world that scorns the ideals of Christ, reduces morality to the level of unbridled indulgence and repudiates the very spiritual nature of man.

There is only one way that we can fail to meet the challenge to reveal Christ in ourselves. That is by failing to remember that we must work to ensure stronger, vibrant, living faith in our personal lives, sanctifying our surroundings and ourselves so as to help improve and elevate our fellow men. To yield to the atmosphere of worldliness in which we live or to the blandishments of whatever lessens the image of Christ in our souls would be to invite disaster upon ourselves and to deprive our neighbors of the Christ they long to see.

My dear Catholic women! Ours is an age which offers many and significant challenges to Christian womanhood: on the world front, the challenge of co-existence that summons us to redouble, individually and collectively, our efforts to secure a peace based on the moral and spiritual unity of the family of man; on the level of the Church we are called upon to meet with a renewed sense of spiritual responsibility the challenge of bringing back to the Church its sons and daughters whose steps have wandered from the way laid down by Christ; and, in the life of each of us, more personally and more intimately, the challenge of establishing ourselves as worthy representatives—nay, as living images—of Christ so that He may be known through us.

Many there are who look with pessimism upon the age in which we live, voicing their regret that it fares so badly, prophesying dolefully that it will fare worse yet. Such apostles of pessimism forget that if the world does fare ill, such need not be. It means simply that we have not done enough and that there is so much more work for us to do if it is to fare better, at all!

Saving the world is no task for theorists and it is not easy for practical people. It was not easy for Christ, still less for His apostles. But Christ is with us, by our side, within us—and under such a Leader as He there is no challenge we dare to refuse, no work we need fear to accept, no goal to attain which we cannot set our sights on.

If you take with you from this Congress only one lesson, let it be this: Christ who has overcome the world is with us! It remains for us only to identify ourselves more personally with Him, in our every activity, thought and act of will. His mission is ours;

only we, not Christ, can fail! And when we—with all the rest of Christendom—fulfill the role of "other Christs," faithful reflections of Him, His mission will be fully accomplished. Pray that ours may be a truly apostolic spirit, and that God may find nothing wanting in us!

A Challenge to Catholic Nurses †

Ours is the Church of the Saints. Be ever mindful of that consoling, challenging truth. Walk in the ways of your saints. Take heart from their example. Shape your lives with the lessons they teach.

Since it is your duty to seek inspiration from the lives of the saints, you cannot peruse their glorious deeds without feeling invited to emulate their good example to whatever extent is possible in your own sphere of life. You are thus kept mindful not to lower your Christian standard which demands that you aim at perfection. We are all called to be saints, even if eventually our good deeds may only be commemorated by the Church on All Saints Day. If even one saint by the grace of God and loyalty to His Church can do so much single-handed, who dares set limits to the good which Catholic nurses can accomplish?

Catholic Action is an arduous task. Experience has already taught you that if you follow the will-o'-the-wisp of self-glory instead of wholeheartedly serving Christ, your finest efforts will end in dismal failure for, as the Master puts it: "Without Me you can do nothing!" When discouragement knocks loudly at the door of your heart, when God seems strangely deaf to

† Reprinted from *The Catholic Nurse,* (Boston, Mass.), March, 1953.

your pleadings, when your greatest sacrifices seem all to no purpose, when your own shortcomings appear an insuperable obstacle to your progress, my advice is simply this: go in spirit to the little island of Patmos, stand there humbly beside the beloved apostle John to whom the secrets of heaven were revealed and contemplate anew his description of your heavenly model and patroness. "A woman clothed with the sun, and the moon under her feet and on her head a crown of twelve stars."

Whisper to her lovingly, "Mother, what am I to do?" Her smile will give you new confidence, her wisdom will point out clearly the pathway of duty, her angelic escort will cheer you with the message: "Never underestimate your power as a woman!" From then on you will make progress for you will be convinced that what others have done, you also can do.

We are told that the world needs food, but even more it needs the words that the saints hear from the mouth of God Himself. We are told that the world needs wisdom, but even more it needs the science of the saints. We are told that the world needs work, security, peace, prosperity . . . and all this is true. But more than it needs any creature, more than it needs all created things together, the world needs God's grace . . . the grace that the saints acquire by their prayers and put to work by their deeds.

That is why these are such historic days. It would be accounted a turning point in history if some philanthropist were to pour out riches for the unrestricted use of the citizens. It would be reckoned a day to go down in history if some renowned philosopher or political genius were here to release a successful plan for the peace of the world.

No such plan in the technical or political sense do I bring you. No such riches can we put at your disposition. With Blessed Peter of old, we must say: "Silver and gold we have none."

But it is our exalted privilege, our apostolic duty to bring you those treasures which Blessed Peter *could* and *did* distribute to our forefathers in the faith: the word of God and His grace; the counsels of perfection; the Commandments; the sacraments; the Sacred Scripture; the divine traditions and all the other means and instruments by which the work of the Church is done, by which saints are produced to renew the face of the earth.

Ours is the Church of the Saints because it is the Church of Christ. You are called to be saints because you belong to Christ's Church. So long as you keep the inspiration of the Redeemer, so long as you keep close to Christ who in these moments comes so close to us, then the Church will be made glorious by new Marys, new Monicas, new Elizabeths, new St. Joans . . . and God will be wonderful in the saints among our Catholic nurses.

Making America Catholic †

The nature of your organization suggests to me the general theme of my address. You are devout Catholics. At the same time, you are graduates of colleges and universities. These two facts suggest the apostolate of the educated Catholic to the educated non-Catholic. It is most important because, on the one hand, the educated Catholic frequently keeps the faith to himself as a kind of personal privilege or family heritage; while the educated non-Catholic is usually only willing to learn of the faith from one who shares his intellectual and cultural background.

In calling you to this apostolate of presenting the case for the Church to educated non-Catholics, I might discuss some incidental questions, or the techniques which you should employ. I might comment on some of the difficulties which must be met and overcome, the special psychological difficulties, or the general intellectual, scientific or other problems which are frequently urged by educated non-Catholics as the difficulties which stand between them and the acceptance of Catholicism. I prefer this evening, however, to leave these questions to your individual

† An address delivered at the national convention of Theta Phi Alpha, a national fraternity of Catholic women students and alumnae of colleges not conducted by the Church, held at Swampscott, Mass., September 4, 1946.

study and to develop the wider apostolate of making America Catholic, within which, your apostolate to educated non-Catholics is a specialized branch. Hence our subject—"Making America Catholic."

The late Mr. H. G. Wells decried what he called the "open conspiracy" of the Catholic Church to convert the world and to change the face of the earth. Mr. Wells said many bitter and bigoted things about that "conspiracy" and these things have been repeated by persons close to us here at home. They too have been disturbed by the "open conspiracy" of the Church. We protest against the bitterness with which this Catholic "conspiracy" is misrepresented, as if it were a conspiracy against natural or civil rights or against the good faith and the dignity of others. We protest against the bigotry with which those who profess to despise our "open conspiracy" have banded together in one of their own, to prevent the progress of the Church, and we particularly protest when the counter-conspiracy against the Church uses falsehood, distortion and malicious misrepresentation as its weapons for opposing us. But while we protest against the bitterness and the bigotry, we cheerfully concede the essential accusation: the Catholic Church is engaged in a frankly avowed "conspiracy" to win the world for Christ and therefore to convert all nations to Catholicism.

Your responsibility and mine in the execution of this "conspiracy" is principally directed toward the conversion of America. More than a half century ago Archbishop Ireland stated the essence of our apostolate when he said: "Our work is to make America

Catholic! If we love America, if we love the Church, to mention the work suffices. Our cry shall be, 'God wills it!' and our hearts shall leap with Crusader enthusiasm." We have no special designs on America nor on any other single nation. We frankly pray and preach and hope for the conversion to Catholicism of every nation. We are bound to this position by the logic of our faith: if we sincerely believe that the Catholic Church is the true Church, then it is our clear duty to try, by every reasonable means, to make that faith known and to lead everyone into its fold.

Timidity, human respect and difficulties of every kind must be swallowed up in the supreme desire to share the gift of faith with those who do not possess it. It seems hardly possible that any Catholic today can doubt that he has a duty to be an apostle. Consider, for example, the continued insistence of recent Popes. Said Pope Leo XIII:

"Among the duties that bind us to God and to the Church, let one especially be mentioned—that each one, according to his powers, must exert himself to defend the truths of Christianity and to beat back errors."

Pius X is no less emphatic:

"We know that God commended to each one the care of his neighbor. And so, not only priests, but all the faithful without exception, must labor for the interests of God and of souls."

Pius XI proclaimed the same truth over and over again. Pages could be filled with quotations from his speeches and writings. The apostolate of the laity was the leading motif of his glorious pontificate.

"All are held to cooperate for the kingdom of Christ, because all are the blessed subjects of that reign. All must act, and for all there is a place and a way."

One would have thought that all these exhortations would have been sufficient for loyal Catholic people. Yet the present Holy Father, Pius XII, after nearly twenty centuries of Christianity, finds it necessary to repeat the fact no less than ten times in an encyclical to the universal Church:

"We desire," he writes, "that all who claim the Church as their mother, should seriously consider that not only the sacred ministers and those who have consecrated themselves to God in religious life, but the other members of the Mystical Body of Christ as well, have the obligation of working hard and constantly for the upbuilding and increase of this Body."

Zeal for souls is an elementary Christian duty. It flows from the very fact of the love of God. It is not possible to love God and not to desire His glory; it is not possible to desire His glory and not to work for it. "It is His will that all men should be saved, and be led to recognize the truth." He wills these things through the cooperation of His creatures. The merits of the cross of Christ are to be distributed, not directly by Himself, but only indirectly through the agency of men. This apostolate is the ordinary method of salvation. In this fulfillment is the so-called "conspiracy" of the Catholic Church to win America to Christ.

Within the year certain non-Catholic groups have been attempting to discover the extent to which the so-called "conspiracy" is succeeding. About a year ago, one of these groups published a series of several articles which constituted a report to non-Catholics on the present state of our "conspiracy." The articles were interesting both for what they contained and for what they did not contain: in some points the writers exaggerated our strength, in others they betrayed an ignorance of our position so complete as to render them incapable of evaluating our strength. In attempting to describe the unity, resources and program of our "conspiracy" to convert America, this particular report gave us too much credit in some ways, too little in others. We are nowhere as near the conversion of America as our non-Catholic critics claim.

What is the true picture? How well is the "conspiracy" getting along? As I have said, non-Catholics are unduly alarmed about its progress. A certain non-Catholic ecclesiastic who frequently goes out of his way to expose our efforts recently implied that our plans were proceeding successfully only because we are constantly building up our numerical strength; he implied that the desire to do this is the principal motive for our Catholic position on marriage morality and on birth control. Another non-Catholic said some years ago: "It seems that in another 50 or 100 years the Roman Catholic Church will dominate America. It will do so by sheer force of numbers."

How near to realization are these charges? Does available evidence indicate the progress of our "conspiracy" in America or its frustration?

First impressions would appear to make us optimistic. Within the lifetime of our country as a politically independent nation, the Catholic Church has increased its membership from one in a hundred Americans to one in six Americans. In the latter years of the eighteenth century there were only 30,000 Catholics in the American population of over 3,000,000. Today, in the population of probably 140,000,000 there are more than 25,000,000 Catholics, with more than a score archbishops, well over 150 bishops, many more than 25,000 priests and almost 20,000 churches and missions. We might be more impressed by these figures if other groups had not grown phenomenally here in the United States and did we not remember that our impressive figures are much smaller than the total number of non-Catholics or of those of no religious persuasions. Moreover, we might be more complacent about our numerical strength were it not for sobering indications that our future growth may not be as conspicuous as was our growth from the beginning down to the present generation.

Some factors in our early Catholic growth no longer operate here in America. Immigration from Catholic countries, so powerful a factor in our progress during the last century, is almost at a standstill. Carefully written legislation, totally changed conditions, and the entrenched new nationalism of the United States have removed the welcome sign. We can no longer depend on immigration from Catholic countries for building up our religious strength here in America.

Another factor which seems destined to be less favorable to our growth in the future than it was in the past is that of large Catholic families. While it is generally true that Catholic families still strive to live closer to the law of nature and of nature's God and accordingly tend to be larger, still our Catholic insistence on marriage morality may, in a generation dominated by pagan principles, prove to be a factor diminishing rather than increasing our numbers. Many Catholics may prove pitiably weak in their resistance to the spirit of the times. Our economic system, the planning of our housing projects, our taxation programs and all the rest of American social thinking is founded on the premises of a secular social philosophy, and more often than not that means on the principles of the birth-controllers. This is rapidly bringing to pass a social and economic order in which it will take supernatural strength to remain natural, superhuman courage to be a genuine human, heroic virtue to be normal.

The Catholic, striving in accordance with the ideals of the faith to remain natural, human and normal in matters of family morality, will be in a disadvantageous position, unless something happens soon to rid our national thinking on social matters of the paganism which now dominates it.

The increase of mixed marriages may also be a factor tending to retard the growth of the Church here in America. Some well-informed members of the American hierarchy have long been of the opinion that mixed marriages constitute the chief obstacle to the growth of the Church and therefore the spread of the kingdom of God here in America. One western bishop said: "From the experience which I have had in dealing with this problem, I am persuaded that the mixed marriage is one of the most fertile sources to which we may trace the great loss of souls to the Church in this country. I could give a long list of families whose Catholicity was lost because of this evil."

When serious minds devote themselves to the study of mixed marriages in this country and their effect on the growth of the Church, they express themselves in the most discouraging terms. Here are a few of their typical expressions. "An appalling story of apostasy and loss." "A steady and enormous leakage has been the cost of this particular spirit of toleration." "Mixed marriages have had a devastating effect on the faith in our own country."

A non-Catholic layman, analyzing the mixed marriage situation in the United States, says that the facts regarding apostasy, indifference, and loss of children to the faith do, indeed, seem to justify the attitude of the Catholic Church to mixed marriages. He says: "A church as well as an individual must take measures essential to the preservation of its life. The Catholic attitude, if one grants its major premise, is wholly logical." This non-Catholic layman goes on to criticize the Church for weakening the strength of its attitude by granting exceptions and dispensations altogether too easily.

Another factor which once favored our growth in the United States and which may be less prominent in the future is what we might call "Catholic family loyalty" or a "Catholic family spirit."

Many authorities are of the opinion that the most tragic leakage from the Church in our day is that which results from the defection from the faith of individuals who have rejected all family loyalties, religious ties included. Hence the tragic apostasies of individuals who consider themselves to have outgrown the religious loyalties of their Polish, Lithuanian, Irish, French, Spanish, German or other families. The individualistic approach of non-Catholic liberalism has been a most unfortunate agent in this particular assault on Catholic families.

Other reasons also contribute to the explanation of the large number of fallen-away Catholics throughout the United States. Among these reasons are:

(1) The settlement of Catholics in remote places beyond the normal reach of the Church.

(2) The inadequate supply of competent priests for some national groups.

(3) The many orphans and other homeless children falling into non-Catholic individual, family or social channels.

(4) The lack of adequate Catholic education.

(5) The spirit of indifference to ecclesiastical authority.

(6) The social contempt of educated non-Catholics for their unschooled fellow-Catholics.

The last named consideration constitutes, it seems to me, a particular challenge to people like yourselves. You have a responsibility to carry the Catholic culture into your professional and academic circles, to make non-Catholics respect it and less privileged Catholics grow proud of it. Educated Catholics must, almost alone, meet this sixth difficulty. The other five the whole Church must unite in meeting.

Here in the Archdiocese of Boston we have recognized the problem and tried to do our part. We have established a rural parish program to reach lapsed Catholics who had settled outside the metropolitan area. We are encouraging the legitimate national traditions, devotions and other observances of several racial groups within our jurisdiction; we have fostered and shall foster such schools, religious orders and other ambitions as may be needed in order to keep our national groups loyal to the faith of their fathers. We have revised and shall revise further our social agencies and social institutions to protect the faith of our underprivileged children, and we propose to increase our vigilance and our cooperation in the field of civil and non-sectarian programs to the end that, whatever else they lose through adversity, our children will not lose their faith!

We propose to provide the maximum opportunity for Catholic education under Catholic auspices. For those who still cannot avail themselves of it, however, or who are impelled by any legitimate cause to seek their vocational or cultural education outside Catholic schools, we shall do our utmost in the way of encouraging Newman Clubs, released time courses, confraternities, study groups and special devotions so that it no longer will be possible for a person to be educated in other matters and remain ignorant of Catholicism. The spirit of indifference to ecclesiastical authority we shall attempt to meet by an ever more deliberate effort to identify that authority with the people themselves and the people with it. We believe that the spirit of the Church is the most democratic spirit to be found in any society on earth—and we are convinced that that spirit can be increasingly manifest in the relationship between priests and people, between the faithful and the hierarchy.

I wonder, however, if we realize how slowly the actual work of gaining converts to Catholicism in America is proceeding. The slowness of this work is a definite challenge to groups like yours. Many Catholics have a false sense of progress in convert-making because of the distinguished names of so many of our converts, prominent editors, public figures, and outstanding persons in other professions. But impressive as these names sometimes are, their numbers do not affect the over-all picture.

The fact still remains that in the United States each year there are only about two converts per priest. There is only one solution that I can see: the development of a much more dynamic missionary spirit among educated Catholic lay people. Catholics of today, no matter how sincere their personal faith, are not propagandists. There are hardly enough priests to take care of the wants of our routine Catholic organization . . . much of the work of convert-winning necessarily depends on our educated laity. They are the only ones who can correct the situation arising from the facts that our faith is now being preached from pulpits where only Catholics are listening and defended in Catholic newspapers which few or no non-Catholics ever read . . . We priests are saving the saved; the others must be reached by you if we are going to improve our present discouraging convert figures: about 40,000 converts per year in a nation of more than 25,000,000 Catholics. It would be interesting if we could compare the number of converts with the leakage.

We must consecrate ourselves to a new Catholic evangelism. We must make its instruments worthy of its lofty purpose and its grave responsibility. Catholic books, newspapers, radio programs, street preaching, labor guilds, apostolates of all kinds we shall bless, support, encourage and otherwise implement—but all these must be worthy of our blessing, support, encouragement and sacrifices. If the principles which they preach are confirmed by and reflected in the lives which our people lead, then the tide of conversions will again gain momentum and America will be on its way to Catholicism.

We shall be wasting our time if we undertake to analyze and refute the 10,000 sectarian heresies all about us. We shall accomplish nothing if we bother to meet all the minor attacks made upon us. Too much time has been devoted to the purely defensive apostolate already. We shall make more friends among non-Catholics and strengthen our own ranks if we devote our best energies and the most of our time to being good Catholics. There is no better argument for the truth of Catholicism than a good Catholic. If Catholicism is the work of God, then we will make manifest its divinity by living it before the eyes of friend and foe. Non-Catholics have a right to apply to us and to our faith the test which Christ Himself provided: By their fruits you shall know them!

If our fruits be worthy, those who behold them

will wish to live the same life we live; weak Catholics will be strengthened by our example, and once again there will begin the flow into the Church of all those who with open minds and clean hearts seek God! From the friendships of your college and university days you well know how many there are—how many are honestly seeking God's guidance in their lives. From your own faith you know how much you have to offer them. Do not repudiate your clear vocation; dedicate yourselves to the special apostolate of educated Catholic people: the bringing of Christ's light and love to your non-Catholic associates. As you so dedicate yourselves, know that your priests and your bishops stand ready to help in every way your efforts to build up the kingdom of God, to make America Catholic!

Pray and Plan for Peace †

This is a thrilling occasion. I have rarely in my priestly life felt so convinced of the closeness of God and of the power of prayer as I do in the presence of this throng banded together out of sheer love for God and intent only on prayers for peace.

Peace can only come through prayer. That does not mean that prayer is a substitute for work. Neither does it mean that prayer releases us from the necessity of planning. It does not even mean that we can have peace without bloodshed sometimes, or without patient, conscientious diplomacy always. All these are needed. But we shall not even have these without prayer—and these cannot achieve their desired effects unless prayer inspire them, direct them, coordinate and crown them.

The psalmist said it of old: Unless God builds with them, they strive in vain who seek to build the human city. God enters our lives by prayer.

With God comes peace. Our God is a God of peace. My thoughts are thoughts of peace, saith the Lord, not of affliction. God's will expresses itself in law, not chaos, and law is the basis of peace. God's intelligence formulates from all eternity a plan; a plan

† Address delivered at a meeting of the Catholic Daughters of America at Boston, May 1, 1951.

is the pattern of peace. God's providence is characterized by love, by mercy, by sweetness; these are the attributes of peace. God's power works in the sublime silence, on the calm, secret levels of grace; all this again reveals that God is a God of peace and that peace is a gift from God.

God's Son is the Prince of Peace. Christ came to conquer sin, for sin destroys peace. Christ died to restore life to the souls of men, the more abundant life which includes and intensifies peace.

God's Son resisted hatred, the motive of war; He taught love, the condition of peace. He forgave offenses, the causes of war; He preached pardon, the means to peace. Christ healed discord, the promoter of war; He prayed for unity, the crown of peace. He dispelled error, the fomentor of war; He taught truth, the herald of peace. He strove to cast out despair, darkness, pointless pain and sadness, the spawn of war; He brought hope, light, true consolation, holy joy, the fruits of peace.

Christ was, Christ is, Christ always will be the Prince of Peace. Even when we are driven forth to war, we wage war, if we act in the spirit of Christ, only to bring back peace. God's Son is the Prince of Peace.

God's Church is a supernatural sanctuary of peace in the midst of natural discord. Grace is the principle of the Church's life; by this principle the Church is set apart from the world, lifted above the level of the natural. The law of nature is one of conflict, of rivalry, division and antagonism. The law of grace is one of concord, of cooperation, unity and peace. The kingdom of the world, if left to itself, is a kingdom of chaos. The kingdom of God, in its earthly organization, the Church, is the reign of grace and of peace in the midst of men and nations.

And so the Church is always instinctively on the side of peace. Her prayers constantly breathe her desire for peace. Her Sacred Scriptures always speak of life, of love, of truth and of peace; they mention death, hatred, error and war only to reprobate these and to exclude them from the pattern of the Christian life. The word "peace" recurs repeatedly in the lines of the Scriptures; it is one of the dominant themes of God's book.

So also in the liturgy of the Church: the prayer for peace appears on every page. *Dona nobis pacem!* Lamb of God who takest away the sins of the world, give us peace! This is the most urgent petition on the pleading lips of the praying Church. *Pax vobis!* Peace be to you! This blessing spontaneously springs to the lips of the Church's high priests as they stand before their people. Peace be to you! Then, glory to God in the highest and on earth peace to men of good will! This is the sum of the Church's praise from men to God and of the promise she brings from God to men.

Peace is beloved by all the saints of God's Church. On this first day of May our thoughts turn early and always to the Queen of All Saints, Our Lady of Peace! Could any title be more consistent with the character of the Mother of God, more consistent with our concept of what Mary is and means and offers, than this: Our Lady of Peace? It is impossible to imagine the Blessed Mother on a battlefield save as a messenger of peace, healing the wounds of war and binding up war's bruises.

Last summer in the great Church of St. Mary Major in Rome I stood before the shrine of Our Lady of Peace. Carved out of radiant marble, it is the perfect expression of the relation of Our Lady to the hope of peace. In one hand she offers the olive branch, symbol of our human yearning for peace. In the other arm she holds her Son, Christ the Lord, the Prince and Pledge of Peace. It is as if she were saying to us: "Take whichever you choose—but you will not have one without the other. Take my Son and with Him you will have peace. Seek peace—but you will find it only in my Son. Reject the one or the other—you reject both! You cannot have Christ and seek war. You cannot seek war and keep Christ. You cannot repudiate Christ without repudiating peace. You cannot sincerely desire peace unless you humbly accept Christ!" This is the message of Our Lady of Peace.

Mary is the queen of all saints; and what is true of her in unique degree is true of them all in due proportion. The saints are peacemakers, for they are the privileged children of God. When they are apostles or doctors, they teach the principles of peace. When they are martyrs or confessors, they bear witness to the means to peace. When they are pontiffs or virgins or widows or other types of saints, they proclaim the triumph of peace. Their prayer is always that of St. Francis: Lord, make me an instrument of thy peace!

Hence it is no surprise that the authentic voice of God's Church is always lifted up for peace. "We bless peace," said the saintly Pius X, "we bless peace, not war!"

Armed peace is no peace, the same Holy Pontiff protested, and his protest has been echoed by all who have succeeded him in speaking for Christ in the modern world: Benedict XV, who brought such prophetic gifts to the cause of peace; Pius XI, who proved so valiant a defender of the things that make for peace; the present Holy Father, Pope Pius XII, who is able to make the holy boast, "Read every word of our pontificate. Scan every deed that we have done. You will find nowhere a word or a deed in behalf of war—always the struggle to preserve peace where it is threatened, to restore peace where it is lost."

One of the milestones in the history of human striving after peaceful methods of settling disputes, of mankind's struggle to outgrow militarism and to outlaw warfare, will bear the courageous, statesmanlike word of wisdom and warning pronounced by Pope Pius XII on the eve of World War II: "Nothing is lost by peace, but everything may be lost by war." The word was widely disputed at the time; now only a fool will fail to see that it was and is the essence of sanity, sanctity and sound practical policy. It is still true: nothing is lost by peace, everything may be lost by war!

Rock of peace, the present Pope has been called, and the title is deserved by every count: personally, because of his passionate individual efforts for peace; officially, because, as the vicar of the Prince of Peace, he has given clear leadership in proclaiming God's will and the Church's prayer for peace.

Small wonder, then, that within the month the Holy Father has praised with warm and pointed tribute a group of people who have braved frequently intemperate criticism in order to explore, valiantly and with eager vision, some of the alternatives to war, some of the legal means by which peace may yet be organized on the face of the earth.

Hitherto only war has been organized; only war has had budgets behind it; peace has been left to fend for itself—and even honorable efforts to organize for peace were held suspect.

Hence the timeliness, the intelligent idealism of the Pope's words:

"The Church desires peace, and therefore applies herself to the promotion of everything which, within the framework of the divine order, both natural and supernatural, contributes to the assurance of peace. Your movement dedicates itself to realizing an effective political organization of the world. Nothing is more in conformity with the traditional doctrine of the Church, nor better adapted to her teaching concerning legitimate and illegitimate war, especially in the present circumstances.

"It is necessary therefore to arrive at an organization of this kind, if for no other reason than to put a stop to the armament race in which, for decades past, the peoples have been ruining themselves and draining their resources to no effect."

I myself have frequently felt bound to speak in warning against excessive zeal or impractical dreams in the direction of too hasty acceptance of certain peace schemes. We have all been vigilant against the exploitation of human desires for peace by the disloyal or the anarchist. No one has been more vigilant in this respect than the Pope himself, and all right-thinking men must be grateful for the resolute, clean-cut manner in which the Holy See repudiated the dishonest Stockholm Peace Pledge and like pretended pleas for peace which are really invitations to the chaos that is communism.

But we must be no less grateful for the clear foresight and forthright courage with which the Holy Father commends honest persons who dare depart from old familiar ways in order to discover, if God permits, whether new ways of world organization may not bring us the peace of which we have been defrauded to date.

"What a fund of moral steadfastness, intelligent foresight and capacity for adjustment this world authority will have to possess, qualities more than ever necessary in those critical moments when, in the face of malevolence, people of good will must resort to its authority! After all the proofs of the past and present, would anyone dare to say that the current resources of government and politics are adequate? In truth, it is impossible to solve the problem of a world political organization without being willing to leave the beaten path from time to time, without appealing to the witness of history, to a sane social philosophy, and even to a certain divining of the creative imagination."

It is time that we respond to the call of the Holy Father for courage and clear thinking in the cause of peace, courage to break with outmoded patterns of the past, clear thinking to choose among the proposals for fashioning the future.

To this end I urge that peace plans be made the principal subjects of your study and discussion in round tables, reading circles, study clubs for the months, perhaps years that are ahead. The old saying used to be: in time of peace, prepare for war. There was wisdom in the saying and, properly understood, it still has the truth of clever phrases.

But even more true, certainly more timely and more Christian is another phrase which the old saying suggests: In time of war, prepare for peace! When the passions of war run high and the fever of war renders us eager for the return of normalcy, decency and order—then is the time to direct all the alertness of our minds and the energies of our hearts toward the considerations of better ways than war—of higher levels than battle fields—of more permanent methods than military campaigns as the means of securing our defense for the future and promoting prosperity in peace. These, as the Pope reminds us, will not come in a day and may not come in a lifetime—but come they will, nonetheless!

Catholic Daughters of America, no group on earth has a greater stake in the achievement of a just and lasting peace than you have. As Catholics, you are the custodians of a dogmatic creed and a moral code which comprise the very heart of Western civilization—for Western civilization flows from the ancient faith of Christendom and depends on that faith for the very stuff of its substance.

As Daughters of America, you are the heirs of a way of life which, however imperfect, however open to healthy criticism and deserved rebuke on occasion, still represents the fairest and the most enviable combination of spiritual riches and civic advantages. Both Christian civilization and the American way of life are in danger—and there is nothing a devastating war would destroy which is more precious to you than these blessings to which you are bound by the twin virtues of religion and patriotism, the Catholic civilization and the American civil tradition.

That is why Catholic Daughters of America pray for peace with particular passion, with special understanding of the urgency of their prayers and of the supreme desirability that God grant them mercifully and completely.

Catholic Daughters of America understand as do no other women what the Holy Father meant when he said: "No wise woman favors a policy of class struggle or war. A woman's vote is always a vote for peace!"

So women, especially Catholic Daughters of America, demand of their political and military leaders that they make common cause in the work of achieving peace; that they put aside armament races, universal permanent peacetime conscription programs, balances of brutal power and all the other age-old instruments of war. They demand a chance to venture, with caution, of course, but above all with courage, into new roads and new ways which God's providence is opening before us: ways of charity and justice, of prudence, prosperity and peace.

Let no man say such ways are impossible—that the vision of a world united peaceably in a common reign of law is a mirage, a mere "peace pipe dream." It is only the cynic, the pagan cynic, who pretends that the ways of virtue are beyond our powers—impossible and unsafe.

The libertine says that purity is impossible and that lust is both natural and inevitable. But the libertine lies—chastity is possible, and is attained. The gangster says that honesty is impossible and that rackets are both inescapable and here to stay. But the gangster is wrong—honorable dealings are not merely within the power of all, they are the best basis of practical policy as well as of ideal morality.

The cynic tells us that the organization of society for peace is impossible; that war is fatal and admits of no cure. "To fight is nature." "There is no escaping war." "A world at peace is a poet's idle revery." These are the half-truths of the cynic.

But the cynic is mistaken. Peace is possible. Peace under law is practical. The organization of the world for peace is as feasible as the organization for peace of a city, a commonwealth, a nation or a continent—provided only the same moral motives be operative, the same good will be present, the same graces receive the same cooperation.

Organized peace will come. I know not when—no

man can pretend that he knows. But come it will—since peace is God's will: the will for the triumph of which we daily pray: Thy kingdom come, Thy will be done on earth as it is in heaven.

Peace will come—because Christ has promised it.

A Call to Dynamic Social Action †

The National Council of Catholic Men is an organization of federated societies that consecrates time and ability to the great program of the lay apostolate. The Council is religious in its inspiration, social in its efforts. It is around these two facts that I propose to weave my thoughts tonight.

We hear much in our day about the necessity for social religion and for a religious approach to the social order. This convention celebrates tonight the conclusion of thirty-five years of effort on the part of thousands of Catholic men and affiliated organizations to give their personal religion a social expression and their social service a religious inspiration.

Like all Catholic organizations, the National Council of Catholic Men is based on the conviction that religion is not purely personal, but also social; that the Faith does not provide the individual with a means of escape from the world, but with means by which he must serve and sometimes even change the world through the Church. The six thousand organizations affiliated with this National Council appreciate that religion is not a departmental aspect of a

† Address delivered at the convention of the National Council of Catholic Men held in Boston, April 22-24, 1955.

man's thought and occasional activity, but profoundly inspires, influences and motivates all that a man is, all that he thinks, all that he loves and all that he does. It colors not merely his inner personality, but his outward vocation in the world.

The Council, I repeat, represents the collective effort of many societies to realize something, at least, of the social responsibilities of their Faith and the spiritual possibilities of their life's work.

The concept of religion for which a Council of Catholic Men is dedicated is a thoroughly Catholic concept, and since the times are singularly un-Catholic, it is a concept which many contemporary friends of religion do not understand. Many persons, not a few of them well-disposed toward religion, do not see in religion a stimulus to individual and group action; they accept it as a kind of sedative—a calming, consoling balm to the afflicted spirit—and little more. Communists once called religion the opium of the people and the devout resented the designation; yet, one sometimes fears that many make of their religion little more than an opiate for their own torments and for the worries of society; they have themselves succumbed to a concept of religion which is far more concerned with the sweet relief that faith is expected to provide, than with the stimulus to dynamic life which is the essence of genuine religious faith.

Our Blessed Lord constantly illustrated His concept of the spiritual life by striking phrases suggestive not of repose or lassitude or peaceful rest, but of energetic action, heroic struggle and dynamic vitality. "I have come that they may have life and have it more abundantly!" "I bring not peace but a sword!" "I have come to bring down fire on earth, and what will I, but that it burn!" "The Kingdom of Heaven suffereth violence and the violent bear it away!"

That a church building should be quiet is undoubtedly desirable; that chapels should exist apart from the crowded ways of life is unquestionably necessary . . . But that the Church itself should be a hushed and hidden thing, that the Church should be aloof, is out of all harmony with the true nature of religion or the purpose of the Church. They miss the whole point of the Faith who permit it to become a mere refuge from reality.

Yet the prevalent defense of religion in our day is based on the premise that the chief effect of the Faith is to offer some other-worldly vision capable of distracting us from this world's depressing realities. Modern psychologists pay religion the doubtful tribute of asserting that it is, at best, a source of psychological relief in a world which is bewildering and intolerable. There is a real danger that in times like ours, times of tragic defeats and bitter victories, this escapist concept of religion may gain ground, and, in an afflicted world, may pass for real faith.

Religion is, of course, a comfort for the troubled mind; it does soothe the hurt spirit as nothing else can do. But it is entirely false to see in religion merely a personal channel for escapism, for distraction from the evils of the world, the evils of sickness and poverty and sin included. Religion should challenge us to meet these head on, to combat them and to conquer them; and the principal consolations of the religious life should come from the victory which religion inspires us to win over evil.

The National Council of Catholic Men recognizes this; that is why it has federated so many units of men throughout the dioceses of the United States. Religion for the Council is an inspiration to collective efforts, not a formula for individual repose.

Another mistaken notion with regard to religion is a characteristically modern notion. It makes the assumption that religion is only one of the many departments of life, even though it be the most important of these departments. To the genuine Catholic man, this notion is unacceptable. He recognizes that religion, if it be truly such, provides a pattern for integral living, a source of energy for total action. It elevates the whole of life to a new level; it gives a new quality to all functions of life, and not merely an additional quality to those which already exist. The Catholic man recognizes that his religious life is not divided into two series of activities, one natural as shaving, whistling or performing daily duties in business or professions; and the other supernatural as praying or receiving the sacraments. By virtue of the supernatural life, on the contrary, natural activity is caught up into a higher and wider sphere of reality. It is given new meaning and purpose, new quality, new worth, new and eternal implications. So the Catholic man does not departmentalize this supernatural religion and his natural vocation. The work by which he wins his bread is also the work by which he wins eternal life. The most simple service he performs for his fellow-man acquires from its religious overtones a dignity which makes it acceptable to God. The man living by this concept of his vocation makes of every day the Lord's Day; he does not go to church on Sunday to find God; he goes to work to find God all week, and goes to church to enjoy God and to learn more concerning how God may be found in every word and work of his daily life.

Organizations of such men never possess a purely negative attitude toward religion. Many, however, have fallen victims to this negative view. When they examine their consciences with regard to the virtue of charity, for example, they are more inclined to wonder about whether they have been guilty of sins of thought, word or deed, than they are to measure their positive growth in that flaming virtue of charity which is the very stuff of the Christian life, its positive source of richness, of growth and of dynamic action in the man born again by grace.

I suppose that one reason why the moral side of religion has become negative for so many is the fact that the Ten Commandments are couched in terms of negation; they tell us what not to do, and so taken by themselves, may easily occasion a false emphasis in our understanding of moral perfection. But the prohibition of sins does not suffice for the production of perfect men. That is why the Old Law, though good indeed, was imperfect until Christ supplemented its negative prohibitions with positive precepts. Our Blessed Lord never said to His disciples, "Thou shalt not hate," "Thou shalt not doubt," or "Thou shalt not deny." He said: "Thou shalt love the Lord thy God with all thy heart and thy neighbor as thyself." He said: "I was hungry and ye gave Me to eat, thirsty, and ye gave Me to drink; I was a stranger and ye brought Me within; naked and ye clothed Me; I was sick and ye visited Me, in prison and ye came unto Me."

So religion must never play the part of a mere policeman in our lives; it must be the dynamic, positive, impelling center of our lives. To produce the best results from this dynamic force we must organize to become lay apostles in our parishes. We must unite to produce results in our respective dioceses. But to get anywhere with television and radio programs, or with the fruitful studies of the various departments of the National Catholic Welfare Conference, which is the voice of the American hierarchy, or to solve problems of a national character, we must coordinate programs and join a united front of nationwide strength and leadership. That is the purpose of the National Council of Catholic Men.

It recognizes the truth that religion is not a system of negative prohibitions, but of positive, constructive obligations, privileges and opportunities for laymen to serve God and His Church as only they can do it. Its units have always understood that religion can never be purely personal; it must always bear social fruit on every level. They have recognized the fact that the spiritual and rapidly increasing technical complexities of modern life require every society of Catholic men to extend Catholic Action in wider fields than parishes and dioceses.

Furthermore, through its federated organizations the National Council of Catholic Men looks forward not backward. It constantly looks to the future and is solicitous for the welfare of the Church not only in the present but in the years to come. Its programs and works all give a place to the generation that is coming along. That is a Catholic attitude—the attitude that the future may be less pleasant, sometimes, than the past, but that it is always more important. We reflect that attitude, for example, by our interest in national legislation, national problems, national programs that pertain to the welfare of the country, to the freedom and the rights of the Church.

Every Catholic unit of the National Council of Catholic Men should be an architect of the future, not a eulogist of times gone by. Too many religious people live in the past; too many are preoccupied with the thoughts of wonders which, however great, are now dead. The thirteenth, greatest of centuries, is a typical catch-phrase of a certain Catholic point of view. Why this should be, I do not know. It is not the mood of the Church; for the Church every century has the greatest of opportunities, and all times are God's. The Church always looks to the future—and cherishes the past chiefly for what it can teach us concerning how to build the future, and build it better and more divinely than it was built in the past, to look to the future and always to live for the future.

But, again, we cannot function alone. We must organize on every level and be federated in a national way. If years ago the Catholic men behind the Iron Curtain could have been warned of what was coming, the Church today probably would not be in chains. Yet, who knows? Perhaps they were warned but were not active. Perhaps they were warned but not organized. Perhaps they were warned and did organize, but not in a national way.

I am trying to visualize the future so that we at least shall not be caught unprepared if night should fall upon our land.

Our country as well as our Church needs us. No one knows if we are destined to suffer the disaster of a third World War. All that we can say with certainty is that those who cry out most loudly for peace will be the aggressors if war should come.

Never forget that the largest military forces in the world are controlled from Moscow, where the pledges are composed.

If these forces are ever in control of the world, we will become a nation in chains and religion will be suppressed; the leaders among the clergy will be imprisoned and the flock will be left without shepherds. It will be too late then to present a united front.

No one knows what powers and influence are ready to deprive us of our religious and civic rights here at home. We must be organized lest disaster overtake us. True, we are organized in a fashion. We have wonderful groups of men and women of all types doing God's work for souls and country.

But their strength is weakened without a common national bond of unity. Federation is the answer. And that, my friends, is the logic and the study behind the National Council of Catholic Men.

Four

THE POWER AND RESPONSIBILITY OF THE PRESS

The Apostolate of the Catholic Press †

When the apostles preached from the housetop on the first Pentecost, when their very shadow healed the sick, when their example inspired total strangers to embrace a willing martyrdom—they marvelled, ladies and gentlemen, at the terrifying power entrusted to their hands. Personally weak, and even sinful men, not as learned as they might be, not as pious as they should be, they were made wielders of the irresistible "fisherman's net" with a world as mighty as the ocean in which to ply their trade.

Two thousand years ago, indeed, men must have felt that God's confidence in our race had reached its climax. I wonder what they would have thought could they have foreseen this day when a man's thoughts can fly from mind to pen; from pen to press; from press to paper; and from paper to the public eye—almost in less time than it requires to recite the process!

The superstitious pagans would have worshipped us as gods, who could do such wonders; the simple among the Christians would have reverenced us as saints, us to whom such extraordinary opportunities to multiply God's word have been given. And they

† An address delivered at a meeting of the Catholic Press Association at Boston, May 23, 1946.

would have taken for granted that zeal and that humility which we, in our noblest moments, should seek to make characteristic of our stewardship of the printed word.

Speaking to you on the apostolate of the Catholic Press, I consider that in a real sense I speak as one of you. From my earliest days, I have been fascinated by the power of that profession which is yours. If anybody is, I am a "printers' bishop." I have let flow my fair share of printer's ink. To me the rolling of a press is as much music as the harmonious sounds that shake the classic roof of our justly celebrated Symphony Hall. Throughout my years I have encouraged every form of dignified publicity that might help to bring the Word of God to men. I have never turned a worthy writer down. I have been willing to subsidize any sentence that had a subject and a predicate—even implied. I have made pamphlets a veritable means of crusade in behalf of all the causes identified with the Faith which it has been my privilege to serve. I have done these things because I feel that this wonderful power of the press, which was not available to our predecessors in what we sometimes feel were more favored times, has not been given us by God except for the advancement of His kingdom.

If I seem to address myself directly to the members of the Catholic press and to ignore the vast majority of persons present in this gathering, it is only because all here tonight desire me, they commission me, to express their feelings towards the *greatest single agency*—apart from grace and the sacraments—which makes it possible for men of the present day to build the spiritual structure which is the Church, a structure designed with divine vision by God's own Architect on the hills of Galilee long centuries ago.

When we as children first read the words of the classic author, "Verba volant, scripta manent," we did not sense the implications of the phrase. "Words fly away; what is written—remains!" This is at once a warning and a challenge. All that we say in speech expires with the breath that uttered it; what we incorporate, give living body to, in print—that endures forever.

It is a warning—write well! It is a challenge—fight honorably! As writers on the best of themes, and as fighters in the best of causes, I salute the representatives of the Catholic press here tonight! I gladly offer you this soothing hearth of true faith—which is Boston—as the focus of your deliberations, however spirited. I welcome here every honest Catholic controversy, because, as at least our own people know, I am as willing to be led as to be a leader in any good cause.

I welcome with particular affection those elders among you, who in the days when my lips were, like those of the young and inarticulate Isaias, as yet untouched by the flaming coal, were urging with eloquence and energy the glories of our Catholic Faith—often enough, to a people who had ears but would not hear.

I welcome the very young among you, the subordinates, the assistants, the associates—or whatever name you have above your door—who sometimes weary of the task of polishing your armor, so anxious are you to venture forth as leaders in the fray.

I welcome gladly the ladies, members of the press, who bring to Catholic journalism what good women bring to every field of human effort, a gentle, refining instinct, and a consecrated devotion that would put members of the self-styled "'stronger sex" to shame.

Boston, historically, is a city that knows more of pens than of ploughs. Deprived of the rich acres of our western neighbors, our predecessors sowed, and labored, and harvested in the fields of thought. Some years were years of plenty which we were able to share with the world; others were years sufficient for our own needs; others still were times of famine. Yet the diligence of the laborers has always been unquestioned. Our own paper, *The Pilot,* is a Catholic symbol of the journalistic history of our city.

In 1829, twenty years before it could be written that there was only one statue of Our Lady in all London, *The Pilot* first issued from a creaking press. And looking over the shoulders of those sturdy Catholics as they read its pious prones were neighbors who remembered when Washington reviewed a rustic band beneath an elm tree in Cambridge, and who were still reminiscing about the visit of the charming Frenchman, the Marquis de Lafayette.

And our European confreres in the Faith applauded. Reading stray copies of this brave young newspaper as it occasionally found its way abroad, they must have reverently received it as almost the first documentary evidence that the Faith—their Faith and ours—was here to stay.

When *The Pilot* had passed out of the experimental stage, its columns unfortunately had to be dedicated to the chronicle of a calamity in Ireland scarcely equalled by the historic plagues of Egypt. In Egypt centuries ago, God had afflicted His avowed enemies; in Ireland He was laying a cross on those He loved. When the great famine came, all Ireland resounded with a litany that must have evoked the presence of Patrick and of Brigid: "Thanks be to God!" And then, with the fearless energy of those in the state of grace, hundreds of thousands of those afflicted people embarked on the bosom of the Western Sea.

It is to no purpose here to speak of the Irish emigration to America, or, in those days, to almost the only America they knew—Boston. But consider their delight upon arrival on an unknown and somewhat hostile shore at a New England which in its pompous pride offered little variation from the Old England that they knew all too well—consider their delight to find here, in the cold majesty of print, the truths of their venerated faith boldly proclaimed in the pages of *The Pilot*. If you should have occasion to visit the treasures of our glorious Public Library, across the street from here, you will find the very page from which they read. For the complete files of our diocesan paper are carefully preserved in that splendid institution. We have, moreover, had the complete file microfilmed for the convenience of historians and other students.

The further history of *The Pilot* reflects the history of the Irish people and of Catholic people generally in "the States." *The Pilot* uttered its prayer over

Lincoln when he was fatally wounded on Good Friday night in 1865. It spoke impartial valedictory over the heroes of the Blue and of the Gray. *The Pilot* printers sought eagerly in their fonts for letters large enough to herald the great day when this was made an archiepiscopal see, and my venerated predecessor, John Joseph Williams, received the first pallium that ever ventured toward these "stern and rockbound coasts." Then Boston came of age.

The Pilot saw great days, sees great days, and, with God's help, will see great days. But when I say "*The Pilot,*" I really mean the Catholic press, of which the printed organ of any particular diocese is only one small part. I esteem as much, read as willingly, and support as heartily any and all of our Catholic publications as I do our own. Catholic truth is a universal fact; only its minor manifestations can be local. Side by side in this great work of revealing it to men, we must all depend on one another.

We need not fear or be disappointed if any Catholic tells us that he prefers another Catholic paper rather than our own. In divers tongues were spoken the wondrous works of God; we never know in what particular idiom the Spirit of God may speak to a particular soul. For this reason I am enormously distrustful of laborers in the same vineyard who turn aside from their work to suspect and impugn the motives of each other. Thank God the Catholic press in this country has been wholesomely free of this pernicious "boring from within."

I am so pleased, ladies and gentlemen, by this opportunity of paying my respects to you who shape the thinking of so many millions of our brethren throughout the country that I could go on and on to glorify the high vocation to which God has called you. Glory is sometimes defined as "clara cum laude notitia," that is, clear knowledge of the excellence of anything accompanied by appropriate praise.

Having indicated how great would be my praise could I but linger over it, let me proceed to suggest what a "clear knowledge" of the position and opportunities of the Catholic press implies.

The Catholic press is a number of buildings, machines, filing cabinets, and people. But these particular buildings have a kind of consecration about them; like a church, they stand out in the community. These machines sing a kind of sacred song—we cannot imagine blasphemy or obscenity issuing from them. These filing cabinets have the look of reliquaries, they contain sacred history and blessed records. And these people—they have sanctifying grace, and they subtly turn buildings, machines and cabinets into almost sacramental instruments of supernatural good.

The Catholic press, then, can be called an "angel" in the root sense of a messenger from God to men. Like Gabriel of old, it still brings to men the tidings brought to Mary; like Raphael, it proffers to afflicted society remedies of heavenly efficacy and is the faithful guardian of the way; like Michael, it is a prince among the heavenly host, it defends us in battle and it aspires to be our protection against the snares of the enemy on the many fields of modern thought and debate.

The four evangelists are so called because they are the "messengers of good tidings," the "angels" of blessed news. With all due reverence, the writers in the Catholic press can be called the evangelists of the present day; the weekly and the monthly issues of your publications, although surely not divinely inspired, may be called the scriptures of our times. Everyone will know what I mean when I call the Catholic press the fifth gospel, the gospel which records the activity from day to day of Christ and His Holy Spirit in the world.

If I have up to now addressed you in the character of members of your profession, let me now under the aspect of one not immediately connected with its routine daily work attempt to tell you what our Catholic public expects of its journalistic experts.

The supreme member of the Catholic non-journalistic public, our Holy Father the Pope, speaks of the press as one of the strongest forces for good or evil in the entire world. "The press must be undeviatingly loyal to the truth," says His Holiness, "lest its tremendous influence be exercised amiss." Skillfully as always he distinguishes between two aspects of this truth, pointing out by implication a way in which truth itself can be used as an instrument of falsehood, a propaganda device of which the right and the decent have often been the victims. "The truth of which we speak," says the Holy Father, "is the *truth of vision,* by which you see the events as they actually happen, and the *truth of presentation* by which you report faithfully the events as you have seen them and interpret them by no other standards than those of justice and charity."

The Pope is speaking to journalists in general; of Catholic journalists he and we expect, indeed we take for granted, just such loyalty to truth. However, there is always a subtle danger in using methods which necessarily are of this world that we be tempted to imitate the world's way of using them. Leo XIII, in opening the Vatican archives to scholars, solemnly warned them: "The Church has no need of lies." In our Catholic press we have no need of lies, of half-lies, of unverified facts, of suppositions glossed over as uncontroverted realities, even in defense of truth. You, ladies and gentlemen, have no need to have this admonition addressed to you; we merely state it to show the world under what banner we work and fight.

What if the Catholic press never startles anybody? What if our headlines never shock anybody? What if our editorials are so frequently a variation on an old theme? It is the theme that is old, yet ever new. Hence, whatever crumb of Catholic doctrine an inquirer may come upon in a discarded issue of a Catholic publication, we have infallible assurance that that crumb still holds its nourishment for the mind and soul. You who utilize one of man's greatest inventions to advance the progress of eternal things need datelines only to satisfy convention. History, whether made in this hour, or a thousand years ago, is equally valid, equally inspiring, provided that they who record it have truth of vision and the truth of presentation.

The truth of presentation, being a matter of conscience, needs only such noble hearts as have distinguished our Catholic writers since the first of them took up his pen. But the truth of vision, being a matter of actual observation, depends upon opportunities, acquired skill, persevering effort. It is for you, ladies and gentlemen of the press, to develop the skill, to provide the perseverance. It is for all of us, however, bishops, priests and people, to see to it that you have the widest possible opportunity to pursue your vocation. We must subsidize, if need be, worthy correspondents in distant places; we must support bureaus and news centers; we must, even at the cost of sacrifice, provide for our writers and publishers every possible advantage known to their profession in this modern world. I am glad to tell you, face to face tonight, that the Archbishop and the Archdiocese of Boston stand ready to aid your episcopal leaders in this direction.

Everyone is aware, and in no place more so than here in Boston, of the immense exertions of scholars and investigators who devote years of their lives and go to the ends of the earth to discover by excavations and monotonous inquiry some fragmentary truth from the distant past. These learned expeditions are joyously satisfied if, upon returning home, they can add even a paragraph to the recorded history of ancient times. How much more vital, how much more necessary, it is, in these days when the "truth of presentation" is so often forgotten, that we have means and men capable of looking for us, capable of listening for us, wherever history is in the making.

The secular press could not exist without such correspondents; the Catholic Press has no miraculous powers enabling it to dispense with such a logical and obvious means of gathering its news.

I hope, therefore, that your association will consider means to provide us with the best possible coverage at home and abroad. "At home" and "abroad" are neighbors now; it has become trite to say that the world is growing smaller and smaller. Oceans and mountains are no longer protecting walls making us impervious to events beyond them. For some reason, in God's wise providence, a time has come when every joy or sorrow is shared by all the world. Under these circumstances it is now more imperative than ever that we be well informed, and quickly informed of happenings all over the earth. It is neither safe nor desirable that our Catholic "truth of presentation" remain dependent upon the vision of others. We must learn through Catholic agencies the news, good or bad, of the Catholic family all over the world. We have discovered that we cannot depend on neutral or secular agencies for fair and complete accounts of the fortunes of the Faith. Hence our need for you, greater than ever before.

Your office as Gabriel, healer and guide, is the next to be considered. Among the most learned and consequently the most respected, of human professions is that of the physician. How much the more is that of a healer of the soul. The priest in the sacrament of penance is such a healer. But the Catholic press has it in its power to extend a thousandfold that expert counsel he gives there preparatory to forgiveness. The press can touch proud hearts that might for long years avoid the sacred tribunal. The press can prevent pure hearts from needing the remedies of that tribunal. The press, by a prompt and exact diagnosis of the evils of the hour, as each arises, may check an epidemic of vice and sin, and isolate the contagion of malice and immorality.

We have three great agencies for the propagation of the principles of wholesome living among the masses of the people: the pulpit, the platform, and the press. In the pulpit, as often as not, we are "saving the saved"; at least, our efforts are limited to those who are physically present in a church. On the platform, usually, we are addressing the well-disposed; interest of one kind or another has prompted them to sit before us. But the press is sent out into the "highways and the byways" to fall under we know not what eyes, or how many—friendly, indifferent, hostile, all alike.

For a long time a man may fight against the advice of his physician. But sooner or later, the deep-seated instinct of self-preservation forces him to seek some remedy for his ills, some solution for his problems. Thus the persistent voice of Catholic truth, perseveringly repeated by our press, week by week, month by month, may sooner or later cure the ills of countless souls and direct unto the Good Shepherd many of the flock who wander and who otherwise would perish.

No one practices medicine, no one in civilized communities is allowed to practice medicine, without a long and arduous preparation. Seldom can our

Catholic press be accused of harboring "quacks" or dealers in patent medicines. Our editors and writers are men of education and experience. When the intricate concerns of the faith are in dispute there is always a priest at hand, a trained theologian selected by lawful authority for his expertness in his field. Our Catholic laymen, members of the press, prove their genuinity, in both faith and morals, or they are dismissed. My constant prayer is that we may develop more and more of such people for the needs of the future. Theologians can be trained in journalism; journalists can be instructed in theology. The blend of these two disciplines should give us the most efficient possible apostolate, the apostolate that gives timely expression to the eternal good news of the Gospel.

Lastly, there is your great office to emulate St. Michael. With him we associate notions of loyalty and heroism. He is the captain of heaven's "noble guard." It is he whom we ask to defend us before we leave the altar after every Mass. He is our white knight—without fear, without reproach.

Curiously enough, since the invention of the printing press its use as an agency of controversy and of battle has never been lost sight of. Born in an age of bitter struggles, it constantly betrays the troubled circumstances of its origin. Even the Catholic press, as we now know it, has not always been free from the temptation to deal the devastating blow. There is a momentary thrill in giving vice its name; in calling a spade a spade. There is a very worldly satisfaction in finding the deft phrase that puts an adversary to flight. Our papers love to "score" some person or "flay" some idea. We are great "prosecuting attorneys."

But in this moment of our history we have much more important things to do than winning mere polemical victories over critics and adversaries. We can safely forget the opposition for a while and devote our best energies to building up for ourselves a positive case. We can do no more important work than that of teaching our own. Let the practical consequences of their own errors serve as the best refutation of our enemies.

How will the press best meet its duty to teach our own? What must our press teach them? It must teach them, above all things, a keen discernment in the analysis and the understanding of the times. It must teach them the art of "editing" all they hear and read and witness. It must teach them to distinguish what is accidental from what is essential, what is transient from what is permanent, what is temporary from what is eternal. In the words of a great French cardinal, one of the most heroic men of God to come through the recent war, we must teach our people to distinguish mere devotions from devotion itself, mere decorations from the altar itself, mere candles from the God of Light, mere cobwebs from the true lines of the sanctuary. We must not permit our people to confound mere statues with the Blessed Sacrament, mere groups of Catholics with the Church itself; we must distinguish politicians from priests, propagandists from prophets, bank notes from titles to heaven. We must never confuse hatred for men with zeal for God, lies with truth, thieving with business, slavery with civil obedience, atheism with progress, calumny with patriotism, vengeance with justice, man with God, the State with the Absolute.

In this titanic work of clarification and instruction to which we are called by the times, the press has not merely a work to do, it has *the* work to do. See that you do it well. God grant you grace to write well of Him in times that know Him not! Then may you see Him face to face, for a personal and happy interview, when your last line is written, when your last page is "put to bed," and when you get your final–and eternal–assignment!

The Responsibilities of the Journalist †

For the second year we gather on the feast of St. Francis de Sales to ask the special blessings of God on the men and women who, in their varying capacities, are part of what is simply called "the press." St. Francis, who was a prolific and persuasive writer, long ago was named the patron of the press because he so remarkably appreciated the power of words to impress and influence the human mind. In our days of organized propaganda we know to what lengths this power is used. Its most authoritative voice is the daily press. Everyone who assists in the production of the present-day newspaper and indeed even those who buy the paper must feel that they have made some contribution to its existence and in this sense at least bear some responsibilities for its effects in the community.

Every weekday in the United States of America more than fifty million newspapers are printed and distributed. On Sundays a little less than fifty million papers come into the homes of America. If we can presume that more than one person reads each paper it is easy to conclude that many people, per-

† Address delivered at the second annual Journalists' Mass in the Oratory of St. Thomas More, Boston, January 29, 1955.

haps even most people, actually read more than one paper a day.

The newspaper has become so much a part of our daily lives that we feel somehow lost when, for one reason or another, we are without it. Even when its delivery is delayed we are annoyed and in many cases we become so attached to a certain paper and its style that we find it difficult to read the news with the same interest from another source.

Once upon a time people worried about what radio would do to the newspaper and more recently there was a certain anxiety about the effect of television. As matters turned out both radio and television have merely opened up new subjects for newspaper treatment; the approach of these other media to the problems of the news has been interesting and effective in many ways but it has not replaced, and can't conceivably replace, the newspaper in the modern world.

The ordinary citizen finds in his newspaper the history of his own time unfolding before him. He sees its triumphs and disasters, its enthusiasms and its worries; he finds there an explanation for the complexities of international life; he finds, too, a description of the decisions affecting the life of his own nation; he learns the meaning of the happenings in his own community.

In the pages of his paper he becomes acquainted with his neighbors, with those who present a program for human betterment and with those who find it necessary to criticize the existing order of things. The reader of the daily press meets all kinds of people in its pages—the man in political life who, as an elected official, seeks his support; the religious leader, who recalls for the edification of his people the spiritual values of man in society; the professional man in law or medicine or education who informs the public on the area of his interest. Along with these he meets all those who as each day passes "make the news."

Of course he also meets in his daily paper the troublemaker, the lawbreaker and the victim of accident and personal tragedy. He finds there also, and sometimes in lurid detail, that special brand of person that defies convention or decency or simple propriety merely for the sake of notoriety and personal attention. Even if in somewhat uneven terms, the ordinary citizen reads in his paper the history of his own days, and the historians, who one day will record from another time the story of our years, will look to the newspapers for the most accurate and most detailed description of the life we led, the ideas we had, and the ideals we sought.

Against this background it might be salutary to call to our attention this morning the responsibility of the press in the face of the tremendous influence it holds over the minds and the manners and the morals of men. Certainly no one can read his newspaper without being affected by it—if it is no more than mere information that is added to a human mind, if it is only a point of view that somehow seems to be attractive, if it is only impressions, not even clear ones, that somehow seem worthy of his attention. The reader at any rate carries away from his perusal of the paper something which he did not have before, something which makes him at least in a little way a different person. In this sense the newspaper might be said to *form* as well as to *inform* its readers. It shapes, in fact, the society which it serves.

When newspapers are excited and noisy and frightening, their readers cannot help being, in turn, enkindled and aroused to a similar kind of hysteria. When the newspapers are lurid and suggestive and improper, they plant the same subtle poisons in the mentality and emotions of their readers. When the newspapers are inaccurate and partisan and prejudiced, they prepare the ground for faulty judgments in the citizens they serve.

But when newspapers are alert and accurate, when they are fair and impartial, when they are efficient and dedicated, these virtues too are reflected in the dispositions of the citizens who read them. It is obvious, of course, that there is no such thing as a perfect newspaper any more than there is such a thing as a perfect man, but we all strive for perfection. We work toward perfection as toward a goal and, unless we set for ourselves a goal so high as to seem to be beyond our reach, we will, in fact, always fall below the good that we are capable of doing. When a paper is satisfied with itself, it is taking its first step backward, for the best minds will know that even as men we generally fall short of what we should be.

We know that our first responsibility is to truth and we try to serve it with a genuine and sincere heart. Every newspaper and periodical, whatever its immediate objectives, can find justification for its existence only in the part which it can play in keeping the public accurately informed and in molding public opinion along the lines of an objective and constructive philosophy of life.

We are rightfully indignant as we learn of the shameful subservience of the press behind the Iron Curtain to the enslaving power of the state. We would certainly offer vigorous protest, were we to be ordered by the highest authority in the land to misrepresent and distort facts simply because the truth of facts would be dangerous for the continuance in power of the existing government. We would hardly regard it as consistent with our constitutionally guaranteed human freedom if we were required to convert the resources of American journalism into agencies of propaganda, whose criterion of truth would be governmental decrees and whose norms of morality would be established by the varying whims of ruthless dictators.

Let us keep this terrifying possibility in mind as we reflect upon the rights and functions of a free press in a free country. There is a tendency in every group to isolate itself from the total community of which it is an integral part, to allow selfish and partisan interests to motivate its activity and to make expediency and observable results rather than complete honesty and devotion to the truth the standard of success.

Among certain groups of artists, for example, the principle "art for art's sake" seems to indicate their determination to make artistic expression an end in itself rather than a means of helping human nature to realize its noblest yearnings for eternal truth and peace. Again, among many modern scientists there is a tendency toward intolerable glorification of scientific progress which we might similarly characterize as science for the sake of science alone. I wonder if there may not be a tendency among journalists to follow in practice the principle "news for news' sake," even while protesting that news is essentially and necessarily the reporting of the truth.

It is precisely this inconsistency that can make it possible for the press to lose its freedom. If news value, rather than objective truth, determines the manner of reporting, we are destroying the noble ideals which make it possible to resist the pressure of short-sighted minorities who would use your tremendous power for their own advantage, to the detriment of society as a whole. If we yield to the temptation to trifle with the truth for the purpose of a sensational story, we will have no defense against the unprincipled demands of a growing political despotism which, if unresisted, will bring the press in this country to the sorry state into which it has fallen in countries behind the Iron Curtain.

We have another responsibility. We must have a right understanding of the faults of human nature. Human frailty, in all its ghastly forms, is regrettably a part of each day's news. The reporter must take note of it; he must chronicle the events in which it is involved; he must often, in the interest of accurate and impartial evaluation of the news, stress certain aspects of delinquency and crime which in other circumstances he might be disposed to ignore. For this reason the journalist perhaps finds himself quite frequently in a troublesome dilemma. His reading public seems to demand a certain type of reporting, a certain questionable portrayal of prevalent vice and sin. If he refuses to provide material for the gratification of morbid curiosity, he may run the risk of incurring the censure of employers.

I am merely pointing out the problem; I am well aware that it has no immediate solution, and I confess that I do not know precisely how a future solution can be worked out. Without question the people themselves must bear the greater part of the blame, if for no other reason than that their collective tastes and preferences carry so much weight in the forming of a newspaper's policies.

May I suggest, however, that it is neither impossible nor impractical for a newpaper to contemplate positive resistance even to deeply-rooted and widely prevalent moral depravity. We should not be satisfied to give the people what they want; we should give serious thought to the need of giving them what they need and what will do them the most good. Otherwise we are merely taking our place in a vicious circle of social corruption which will engulf us all together once its whirling madness gets out of control.

From time to time you must seek for a measure that will in some way give an account of your success. Since you are such a potent force in the shaping of society, society itself will reflect your virtues, your ideals, your work and your success. Here in our own community you may look with satisfaction upon what you have accomplished.

Boston and its surrounding area have many special

problems—some of them very serious problems. But this is as it should be. A growing city and a progressive community will always be changing and out of its change will come new situations which raise new questions. The fact that we have problems is no reflection on our city or on ourselves. It is the manner in which we handle these problems, it is the energy and the insight that we use in their solution that give us the key to our true success.

I see in our city, on almost every level, evidences of enlightened leadership and forceful action that with each passing day bring our community closer and closer to the realization of that good society which is our common aim. In this task many forces, of course, are at work—political, economic, social, civic and all the rest. No one of these forces wields a power greater than that of our daily press. Our press has been consistently constructive and positive in its analysis and its presentation of the local scene and its special difficulties. Continue to be so! I urge you this morning to be even more attentive to the evils that, from time to time, seem to flourish in our midst. Do not spare them your strong denunciation when the occasion demands, but be sure, at the same time, to give them your most earnest assistance in a constructive way that will remove the causes that produce them.

This brings me to my final point. We live and work and struggle not merely to survive in the present, but to prepare ourselves for the world to come. We are truly human only if we keep our eyes fixed firmly on the ideals which express the noble destiny of our common humanity, and direct our efforts, shoulder to shoulder with all men of good will, toward the realization of these ideals.

It is an inspiring, if somewhat sobering thought that the words which run so smoothly from your typewriters are received and read, commented on and believed by countless thousands of your fellowmen. Your power is far greater than that of those who hold positions of high responsibility in our legislative and executive bodies. Truly, you are men of destiny. It is not a rhetorical exaggeration to refer to you as prophets, in the literal sense of those who speak to their fellowmen as representatives of God. For truly your power over the minds of men is second only to that of Him who made these minds to know Himself.

To the extent that you become conscious of your vocation, to that extent will you be worthy of the confidence which your fellowmen place in you, and of the mission which God has given you to fulfill. May God give you strength to live and work as lovers of the truth, to build yourselves up into unshakeable columns of resistance against the deterioration of modern society. And may St. Francis de Sales, whose heavenly patronage we invoke today, inspire you all to work unselfishly and perseveringly to further the cause of decency and professional dignity which has prompted you to take part in this edifying ceremony.

Five

MEETING THE CHALLENGE OF COMMUNISM

The Challenge of This Epoch †

I am very happy to be with you. The proof of my desire to be of service is the distance which I have come in order to speak here today. I have left behind me a heavy schedule of graduations, ordinations and religious professions, the extra preoccupations of this particular season. I regret that I cannot stay with you longer—but I am grateful for the opportunity to greet you now and contribute perhaps to the thought and planning of your convention.

I am frank to say that I cannot imagine a more important place for one to be who seeks the interests of the Church than at a convention of Catholic collegians. It is, moreover, particularly important to be present with Catholic collegians who are making their studies and attempting to promote the apostolate on non-Catholic, non-sectarian or neutral campuses.

I say that for a particular reason.

In a sense you people should be admirably equipped to understand better than most certain of the special problems of the Church in the modern world. Like the Church, so you are surrounded on every side by non-Catholic values and occasionally

† Address delivered at the mid-century convention of Newman Clubs held in Cleveland, Ohio, June 15, 1950.

anti-Catholic forces. You should be able to evaluate from the vantage point of your particular experiences something of the general problem which confronts the Church herself in a secular environment which is in turn hostile, indifferent, and unsympathetic, or, in any case, different.

Your Catholicism, nourished by the Newman Clubs, should be of great service in enabling you personally to meet your particular problem, the problem of being part of the non-Catholic collegiate world and yet, in a legitimate sense, above it, not entirely of it. Conversely, you should be particularly qualified to help Catholicism, nourished by your zeal and your experience, to fulfill its divine commission to spread the faith in a society so often and in so many ways alien to her spirit, her genius and her culture.

Mid-Century Year provides an appropriate opportunity to appraise what is being done and what must be done to render more secure the position of the Church and to extend her saving influence in our modern society, on its campuses, in its every area.

This is a good time to appraise the relative influence of the Church as compared and contrasted with that of her principal adversary in the modern world, her principal competition in the age-old struggle to persuade the minds and win the hearts of men. That adversary and competition, as I need not say, is the new religion of the Russian East: communism.

Let me state quite candidly that my conference to you today is largely what the scholars would call a "derived" contribution. I have based the first part of what I propose to say on a remarkably thoughtful article which appeared just two weeks ago in *The Commonweal.* It was entitled, "The East Looks to the West," and I refer you to the complete text for your further meditation on the essential point I intend to make.

The article was written by Mr. Charles Malik. Mr. Malik is the Minister to the United States from Lebanon. Some of you may remember how ably this highly intelligent and zealous representative of one of the smallest countries in the world valiantly spoke up for Christian values and Christian principles in the face of the organized opposition of the most powerful nations in the world on the Human Rights Commission and at other meetings of the United Nations. Those who remember the remarks of Mr. Malik on the true basis of human dignity, on the inalienable rights of the family and on like points during the deliberations of the United Nations Commission recognize in him an authentic voice of universal Christendom, of sound Catholic philosophy, though he is a member of an Orthodox communion.

He is no less a brilliant spokesman of the point of view of the East—certainly of the Christian East, but, I have no doubt, of the entire cultural East as well. His article provides a good basis for the appraisal of precisely what you and I, members of Western civilization, are accomplishing in bringing the leavening influence of the Gospel to bear on the restoration of society. It provides an opportunity for us, representatives of the Western world, to see ourselves as we are seen through the eyes of others, in this case the friendly eyes of an honest critic.

Simply stated, when this particular devout representative of the East looks to us here in the West, he finds much to regret and to lament in his appraisal of us. He does not find as much to praise as he or we would wish.

How do we, the representatives of Western Christendom, look to this outspoken Christian, one of the millions who turn to us to provide the alternative to the oriental despotism which is communism? He frankly declares that there are too many phases of Western life which have become repulsively materialistic. He finds on every side among us a spirit of business and gain, a maddening variety of things exciting concupiscence, an utter selfishness of uncoordinated activity; all this, of course, is not something to attract or to inspire. He warns us that to the superificial observer, to one who is not able to penetrate to the core of love and truth which is still the heart of Western civilization, there seems little to choose between the soulless materialism of the West and the militant materialism of the East.

Most disturbing of all his observations, this friendly but candid critic detects a general weakening of moral fiber among us. He asserts that the great fund of moral strength which has been handed down over the ages is not being creatively replenished in our generation as it must be in every age unless there is to be a terrifying waste of the substance, the very stuff of Christian civilization.

He argues that quality is in eclipse among the

members of your generation and mine. Quantity and size dominate. Not the better and truer, but the larger and physically stronger; these call forth such moral approbation as our Western world still gives.

He warns that the leadership of the West in general does not seem to be adequate to the unprecedented challenges of the age. There is a tragic dearth of men, men who are so genuinely in touch with the hearts of their fellowmen that they only have to open their mouths to be loved and followed. The world desperately cries out for masters—not tyrants, but leaders, leaders who have the voice of conviction and truth that alone can save us. He reminds us that our first prayer should be: God give us men!

There is a corresponding bankruptcy of fundamental ideas. It is in this realm that the struggle for the hearts of men between communism and the West is proving unequal. Communism displays a set of generic ideas—ideas which are false—but ideas in which it passionately believes and for which it is willing to die. There appears to be no comparable passion for our ideas among us in the West. The talk about democracy, freedom, representative government, is woefully inadequate. It is mostly talk and very little more. It deals for the most part with pure form, the external machinery of government, housing, job-seeking and community relations of the most superficial kind. But it is not on the sublime level of ideas which inflame. It does not satisfy man's deepest cravings for friendship, for understanding, for truth and love. It has lost its Christian heart, its Catholic soul, its "guts."

The only effective answer to communism is a rebirth of moving ideas as to how to remove every trace of social injustice without loss of the higher values which constitute the spiritual soul of the West. Communism cannot be met by a mere "nay" or any other mere word. It requires a "yea" with an idea behind it, a "yea" on the lips of convinced men, a "yea" which will do full justice to men's material needs but will at the same time place them in their subordinate position in the scale of human and divine values.

The tragedy of the world today is that the traditions which embody deepest truth are not clearly, sufficiently, responsibly, boldly articulated. They are not articulated because we lack clear ideas of them—and capable men to preach these ideas.

Nor is it sufficient in this cruel century to be happy and self-sufficient. Our friendly critic asks us to step forth and lead. It is not enough to make good institutions and leave it to others to copy them. For man is not merely an ape; he does not only mimic the good example of others. Man thirsts after ideas. Not by bread alone doth man live, but by ideas. What a tragedy if we give the world its bread, and Russia gives the world its ideas!

If the West only exports the silent example of flourishing political institutions and happy human relations, it cannot lead. If the only export is a distant reputation for wealth and prosperity and order, the West cannot lead. Nor can it really lead if it sends forth to others only expert advice and technical assistance. To be able to lead and save itself and others, it must above all else address the mind and the soul. Western tradition, rooted in the glorious Graeco-Roman-Hebrew-Christian-European humane outlook, supplies all the necessary presuppositions for leadership. All the West has to do is to renew the sources of life it already has: rediscover its own ideas, re-create its own men.

The challenge of this epoch is not communism, but it is whether or not Western society, conceived in the joyous liberty of the Greek city-states and nurtured on Christian charity, can still recover from the worship of false and alien gods and return to its father's house—to God—and to its own values. The challenge of the moment is whether modern man, distracted and overwhelmed by himself and the world, can still regain the original integrity of his Christian soul.

Doctor Malik finds many assets on our side as we face this challenge. Both these assets are in your hands as Catholic collegians.

Whatever the weakness of the West, it still has one saving glory: the Church is free, the university is free. It is a great thing to preserve unbroken the tradition of freedom to study started by Plato and Aristotle, and the tradition of freedom to believe emanating from God. Truth can still be sought in our part of the world, and God can still be loved and proclaimed in joy and freedom. And these alone are going to save us. You have access to both. It will not be by pacts, nor by atomic bombs, nor by economic arrangements, nor by the United Nations that peace will be established, but by the freedom of the Church and the university each to be itself. Communism confessed its own failure when it throttled the Church and the university. No one can fight God and win; no one can deny truth and survive.

We must hope and pray that there will develop in the Western world a spiritual renaissance which will rediscover and reaffirm its glorious hidden values, and fulfill mankind's longing for a more just order of things, a more beautiful world, a new heaven and a new earth. Modern man sees before him the possibility of universal plenty for the first time in history, and grasps at any doctrine which seems to promise him the fulfillment of his dream. You, as Catholics with access to God and as collegians with access to truth, should be able to master and state such a doctrine.

Communism is a doctrine of despair. Its only and complete answer, therefore, lies in the Christian preaching of hope. If the Western world can show a way to eradicate the shame and scandal of poverty, of exploitation, of oppression, of greed, without resort to social revolution and class struggle and dictatorship; if it can place these material values in their proper subordinate place within the context of a spiritual renaissance which will be revolutionary without being subversive and which will draw its substance from the infinite riches of the Western Christian tradition, then the threat of communism will vanish, and the specter which now walks the earth will be laid forever. But this answer, I repeat, must come from men, from men with ideas: from men who are Catholics and men who are intellectuals—there-

fore from men like yourselves: men and women who know and love the full Catholic tradition.

I have brought you today the criticism of our society, our so-called Christian society, made by a man from the East who wishes us well precisely because we are Christians—but who fears that we do not display the vitality needed to resist the anti-Christian evil that is communism. With friendly, but keenly critical eye, he appraises us and finds us seriously wanting not in resources, not in virtue, certainly not in anything God need give, but only in an effective disposition to use what we have as it must be used if we are to renew the face of the earth.

Against the background of this critique, I suggest that you of the Newman Clubs appraise yourselves. You are studying sociology. What are you getting out of it which will enable you to help further the kingdom of Christ and resist that of anti-Christ? You are studying history. What lessons is it teaching you out of the past which will enable you to help win the future for God and snatch it from Satan? You are studying languages. Is that study introducing you to a world of thought which you can mobilize in behalf of Christ and use as a weapon against chaos? Are you adding to all these studies the personal study of religion, the personal study of philosophy, at least some study of theology so that you may integrate all your human knowledge with the wisdom of God Himself and thus become God's man or God's woman in the modern titanic struggle between those who are for God and those who are against Him?

What are you prepared to contribute in the way

of ideas to the millions who, thirsting for ideas, turn their eyes Westward—to you? What use are you making of your vaunted freedom to perfect yourself so that you, the free Christian, and not your mere political institutions or your money, may become the inspiration of the nameless hosts of the enslaved who look to the West for guidance?

I repeat—we need men and we need ideas. If any movements should give us both, surely it should be movements like yours: Catholic collegiate movements. Men—leaders of men—should be the plentiful by-products of the Catholic moral code and dogmatic creed. Ideas—ideas capable of moving millions—should be your stock in trade. The Church, the world, the East and the West, join me in my plea that you give us both: good men and great ideas. Don't let us down!

Catholicism's Answer to Communism †

I choose for my subject this evening a theme on which some of you may feel that too much has already been said: Catholics and communism. But I have made the choice because on all sides I see a growing tendency to minimize this spirit of evil, to compromise with it, to be indifferent to it.

More than eleven thousand priests and bishops have been imprisoned, tortured to mental and physical collapse or executed outright in the post-war waves of persecution which have swept the countries harassed by communist rule. This is the casualty list out of a million pastors and prelates who have defended the faith. It is a heavier toll, proportionately, than that taken of the officers in a global war. In the war between religion and materialism, the officers of the faith are marked men. Without arms, they are picked off: innocent and righteous, unobtrusive shepherds tending their flocks.

The sight of prelates, priests and nuns being chained, manacled, and herded off to hard labor in mills and mines is revolting to human justice. To visualize a servant of God placed on a scaffold or stood up against a wall with a prayer on his lips, as

† An address delivered to 10,000 Holy Name men at Salem, Mass., June 30, 1952.

if he were sure that today he would be with Christ in paradise, is to fill the soul with anguish that in this enlightened age men have to be executed for their religious belief.

This diabolical "ism" threatens with equal violence and fatal purpose not only Catholics but all others who love God or who seek to serve Him. It menaces not only our Catholic institutions and the religious institutions of others, but also our most cherished and essential non-religious institutions.

Now, what are the principal evils of communism? (1) It rejects the whole realm of the spirit, of idealism, natural and supernatural alike. (2) It is atheistic. It has no room for the idea of God. It makes no distinction between matter and spirit; between soul and body; it accepts no survival of the soul after death, no hope in a future life. (3) It demands permanent class struggle with consequent violent hate and destruction. (4) It strips man of his liberty, robs human personality of dignity, and removes all moral restraints that check either the blind passions of the individual or the overpowering tyranny of the State. (5) What men call authority is derived in communism from the community as its first and only source. There is no place for appeal to a law or an authority higher than man or the State. (6) All forms of private property must be eradicated, for they are supposed to be the inevitable cause of all economic enslavement. (7) Refusing to human life any sacred or spiritual character, communism logically makes of marriage and the family a purely artificial and civil institution, the outcome of a specific economic system. There exists no matrimonial bond that is not subject to the whim of the individual or of the Red State. Hence the vicious communistic doctrines concerning the nature and rights of the family and the education of children.

Finally, communism today is revealed beyond any manner of doubt not as progress but as a movement of brutal and black reaction. It threatens to reverse the main current of world history and to carry mankind back behind the Christian Era and behind even the Caesars of the late Roman Empire. It represents a throwback under modern industrial conditions, and with the use of the most advanced and devilish psychological techniques, to the slave empires of the Egyptian pharaohs and the Babylonians. It is revealed as a false religion—the religion prophesied by the precursors of Stalin, namely, the religion of the Man-God in place of the religion of the God-Man. The Christian symbol for this kind of religion, which is no religion at all, is Antichrist. In the performance of communism up to this time, and in its even more menacing threat for the future, I believe that we have the most terrible manifestation to date of the spirit of Antichrist.

For all these reasons—reasons based not merely on religious premises but also on purely natural considerations—Pope Pius XI warned the world: "Communism is intrinsically wrong, and no one who would save Christian civilization may collaborate with it in any undertaking whatsoever. Those who permit themselves to be deceived into lending their aid toward the triumph of communism in their own country will be the first to fall victims of their errors. And the greater the antiquity and the grandeur of the Christian civilization in the regions where communism successfully penetrates, so much more devastating will be the hatred displayed by the godless."

It is taking a long and bitter time to drive home by terrifying experience the truth of these assertions. That is tragic enough. But when there are signs that the people of our own country are not fully aware of the evil of communism, or that they are indifferent to it, we must lift up our voice in solemn warning. If we compromise with communism and in any way cooperate with it, we will be eventually absorbed by this spirit of evil.

It is the opinion of many that Catholicism is one of the greatest bulwarks against communism. That is true, and without it all Europe today would be behind the Iron Curtain. Faith, the Christian faith, coupled with the American material aid, has saved France, Italy, Belgium, and other countries, while Spain, by the power of faith and the will to fight, has given communism a death blow within her shores. If every one of almost 400 Catholic parishes in the Archdiocese of Boston functioned with all its capabilities, the seeds of communism would fall on barren soil. The Christian faith, the only power capable of complete victory over red fascism, must flourish in the parish life before it can wield wider influence. Men of the Holy Name, you are leaders of parish life. The roots of your organization must be made stronger on the parish level. If you cannot be a powerful force for Christ—living in your own parishes, you will be helpless elsewhere.

There are three qualities commonly found among Communists which you must acquire before you can save society for Christ. Those qualities are: a burning zeal for the cause of Christ, a profound sense of solidarity with your brethren, and an unswerving loyalty to your Leader, the Eternal Son of God, the Holy Name, Jesus Christ. Humanly speaking, most of our worries about communism would be settled if we had the communistic gifts of zeal, solidarity, and loyalty!

Every communist is a propagandist, a missionary. He has an ardent zeal for his cause and its presentation in a positive manner.

I can gladly listen to any Holy Name speaker who condemns communism and who warns us against the subversive activities of the communist, but I will far more gladly listen to the man who is prepared to give society the positive case for Christianity and who is willing to initiate and be prepared to lead intelligent action for the reconstruction of our social and political set-up. I can approve the actions of those who warn our young people against communist propaganda, but I will applaud far more enthusiastically those responsible for constructive propaganda capable of leading our young people toward social and spiritual security. I can admire the brilliance of those who prove communism theoretically absurd; but I pray God to give us men who by their enlightened zeal in behalf of social justice will make it practically impossible.

You have some appreciation of the solidarity of the communists with their comrades. That virtue you should also imitate. You are dismayed by some of the effects of red solidarity; by the wild-fire spread within a nation of strikes, by the insidious network of communist intrigue which carries revolution under-ground and over-ground from nation to nation when the communists within any nation are active. Catholics and Americans are always fascinated to hear about the red network, the Communist International, the popular front money-raising campaigns, and like evidences of communist solidarity; but it is not enough to expose and to bewail it. I will listen while people tell me of these things, but I shall listen more gladly when they tell me what solidarity they are themselves promoting within our ranks. I may join the protest of our capitalists against communist solidarity when it is aimed against our security, but I shall be more confident of the future of society when I find these same protestors acting in solidarity in our effort to build Christian schools, hospitals, publishing houses, orphan asylums, homes for the aged and other apostolic works, so that we, in a popular front for Christ, can help all our brethren find their proper places in the city of man and in the kingdom of God. I suspect the fears about communism expressed by prosperous people who are not meeting their special responsibilities to the Church and to the under-privileged. It is a sad fact that there have been, and that there are even now some who, while professing the faith, are well-nigh unmindful of that sublime law of justice and charity which binds us not only to give each man his due, but to succor our brethren as Christ our Lord Himself.

Men of the Holy Name, before you tell me about the loyalty of red fascists for the leader, tell me this: what do you do for Christ? How literally have you accepted His call: Come, follow me! What place does He have in your business—your family—your social life—your personal activities? If that place be small, or none at all, you may have a civil right to criticize the Communists, but your criticism will accomplish nothing. If that place be great, if it be what it should be in a devout Catholic, then there will be no need for fear. With half their zeal, their solidarity, and their loyalty, you and your organization can force them into oblivion by winning the political warfare now waging between us.

When we survey the complexity of modern war with its array of intricate armaments—guided missiles, radar, atomic bombs, jet-propelled weapons, and other implements—we know that all of these weapons are at the disposal of the military. They will use them if necessary in their time and place. But also we have on our side the greatest single weapon that can be mustered against an ungodly enemy. If the spirit of faith should permeate all of us as it is permeating the citizens of Poland, Czechoslovakia, Hungary, and Yugoslavia, the forces for Christ, fired with unquenchable zeal, solidarity and loyalty, would be unconquerable! They are defying the atheist. Faith is their weapon. Witness how the enemy is being contained in France, Italy, Western Germany, and Belgium, by the devotional ardor of men of faith.

They are keeping back the scourge. Faith is their weapon. Faith is our weapon. But it must be translated into words and works that are not satisfied with the condemnation of communism, but only with the elimination of the evils that made communism possible.

A few days ago Pope Pius XII received in audience more than 600 pilgrims who had participated in the Eucharistic Congress at Barcelona, Spain. On that occasion the Pope urged the pilgrims to live their daily lives as shining examples of Christianity. He said, "Why cannot you, returning to your country, to your cities and neighborhoods, hold Christ aloft, that all about you may see Him, may recognize Him in your words, your conduct and your whole person, may come to know His teachings, to know that 'the grace of God Our Savior has dawned on humankind, schooling us to forego irreverent thoughts and worldly hankerings, and to live in this present world a life of order, of justice and of holiness,' aware of the inheritance that is yours as God's adopted children through Jesus Christ? Let that thought, dear children, be the measure of the resolution you carry home after this pilgrimage."

In the United States there are almost 30,000,000 Catholics. If all of us—clergy, religious and laity—were suddenly to unite in putting into practice the Holy Father's exhortation, there would be a radical change in the moral atmosphere of this country. Our rich and full Christian living would be as catching as a prairie fire and as irresistible. It would not be possible for others to come in contact with the living fire of faith thus burning in us without being warmed to its glow and inspired to the nobility of Christian thought and conduct.

Men of the Holy Name, accept this challenge of the Holy Father! It is the answer of Catholicism to communism!

A Plea for a United Front Against Communism †

Some years ago, when Nazism first threatened Christendom with the evils which red fascism has now made a reality, there was published a terrifying novel which bore a strange title. It was written by a young German schoolmaster who had fled from the brutal paganism of the Nazi regime. The young teacher had been appalled by the frozen materialism, the utterly godless and soulless atmosphere which, pervading all his nation, had finally invaded his classroom. He had seen clear-eyed, light-hearted, relaxed and confident boys and girls take on the cold-blooded, frozen-eyed, passionless malice of their political masters. He began to note that nothing any longer received from his pupils a healthy, human, normal reaction. Virtue and vice, beauty and grotesqueness, cruelty and kindness, gentleness and bestiality, things divine and things satanic—all alike provoked precisely the same cold, impassive reaction in the generation of boys and girls, de-natured, demoralized and degenerate, who were his pupils, after a few years of official paganism and atheistic indoctrination . . . And all the eyes of these young people, dreadful in their

† An address delivered before a Knights of Columbus forum in Chicago, February 13, 1949.

frozen absence of either remorse or satisfaction, merged in his imagination into one single eye, an eye which from that hour forward haunted him as a symbol of what his generation had become. It was the monstrous eye, lifeless and loveless, the eye of a fish. And then he gave the blandness, the insolence, the calculating, systematic, cold-blooded, passionless perversion of atheistic totalitarianism its true name, the name of his novel, *The Age of the Fish*.

Ours is the age of the fish. The young German school teacher, soul-sick because of what he saw in the eyes of young atheists, who saw their neighbors stoned or raped with neither natural abhorrence nor unnatural delight, beheld only the beginnings of the age of the fish. He did not live to see what you and I are now beholding: the age of the fish, the eye of the fish, the heart of the fish reflected in the pictures which come to us from Budapest, from Zagreb, from Belgrade, from occupied China, from wherever else in all the world red fascism has set up its tribunals, its teachers and all the militia of its atheism, materialism and impersonal faithless, hopeless, heartless tyranny.

Remember the eyes of those who reported to you the confessions of the Russian generals, that they had met with Trotsky in a specific place, when all the world knew that their alleged conspirator had been in a totally different place five thousand miles removed. Remember the eyes of those who released to you the "confessions" of the secretaries and assistants of Archbishop Stepinac, confessions that their prelate had done evil things which even his enemies acknowledged he could not have done, confessions that he had failed to do good things which they themselves had helped him to do and for which they had been praised by Jews and Gentiles, by enemies and allies alike. Then you will be able to understand the eyes of those whose expressionless, mask-like pictures accompany the news stories that Cardinal Mindszenty, a peasant, had confessed to being an aristocrat; that the Cardinal, credited by the Jews themselves with saving tens of thousands of their people by his official actions and of sustaining scores by his personal works of mercy, has confessed to anti-Semitic action; that the Cardinal, once imprisoned for hiding clothing for Jews and for publishing pastoral letters against their persecutors, pastorals which may be read in any major public library, has now confessed that he was not imprisoned for these things and never did do them; that the Cardinal whom two hundred thousand Hungarian men turned out to cheer when he spoke their thoughts in their language less than a year ago, has confessed that he has no understanding of these same people and they no sympathy with him; that the Cardinal, who received permission from constitutional authority to carry on business proceedings of a purely official kind for the essential work of religion (works with which his tormentors boast that they do not interfere), has confessed that he acted in conscious deliberate fraud of his nation; that the Cardinal who distinguished himself for the clearness of his personal and public positions on communism, has confessed that he has been resisting for years the communist campaign without knowledge or understanding of the movement; that the Cardinal after days of mental and moral and physical torture has confessed all these preposterous things and confessed them freely—all this you will better understand when you study certain eyes which gaze out at you from the newsreels, the news weeklies and the daily press, the eyes of the age of the fish.

And yet we have made a little progress. Some eyes at last are beginning to blaze.

When we protested in behalf of Archbishop Stepinac, when others pointed out the crime done Lithuania and the betrayal of Poland, there was no reaction in the eyes of many about us. But now the eyes of all are beginning to stir; some with fear—for they have discovered that what happens in one place can happen here; some with anger—for underneath their hardness they are honorable men and they do not like to discover that they have been hoodwinked, even by themselves; some with shame—for they know the part that our own appeasement has played in making these evils possible; some with determination—for they understand at last that here is an evil with which civilization cannot compromise; some with faith—for they have discovered their consciences and they know that a day has finally come when all who believe in God or man must take a stand against the enemies of both; some with patriotism—for they cannot bear the thought that their land, too, shall go the same way of despotism and disintegration and they now know that there are some already at work in our midst who would force America along that way. Some life has returned to neutral eyes. The age of the fish may be nearing its end. The Calvary of Cardinal Mindszenty may yet yield the Easter dawn of renewed decency and genuine democracy.

But for all this, it still remains true that the communist offensive on the level of religion is frankly aimed first and foremost at organized Catholicism. Note carefully, I say it is aimed at organized Catholicism. Communist agents, both in red fascist governments and among so-called liberals here in America, frequently point out that individual Catholics are not disturbed in their strictly private religious lives. The pathetically misguided ministers who attempted to whitewash the campaign against religion in Yugoslavia came home two years ago with assurances that Catholics were free to wander in and out of church buildings, were seen saying their prayers at wayside shrines and could even, for the moment at any rate, walk with one another to places of pilgrimage. Every hack-writer who defends red policy toward religion sooner or later joins in the chant that under communism individuals are left free to retain whatever religious beliefs they wish and to pray or worship as they personally prefer. It is a routine confusion-technique to point out the phrases in the red fascist constitutions which proclaim individual freedom of worship. But even these propagandists frankly admit the implacable opposition of red fascism to organized religion, to the hierarchy, to the Vatican, to international Catholicism; in one word: to the Catholic Church.

The present strategy against organized Catholicism is all too clear and in it the red fascist dictators of eastern Europe are aided and abetted by scores of fellow travelers in the western world; among them, it pains me to say, even professed religious leaders are occasionally found. That strategy is to seek the separation of the faithful from the shepherds of the flock, to divide the priests and hierarchy alike. How often we hear the phrase on the lips of fellow travelers here in America: We have no quarrel with the Catholic people—our quarrel is with the hierarchy. We recognize the democratic instincts and aspirations of the great masses of the Catholic laity; we only deplore and seek to check the philo-fascism of the few who control the organized Church—conspicuously, of course, the bishops!

It might as well be said once and for all that this kind of talk is, consciously or unconsciously, the communist "party line," no matter who indulges in it. It might as well also be said that, subjectively or objectively, it is a lie. There is no distinction of the kind suggested between the Catholic hierarchy and the Catholic people, between the Holy Father and his priests and his spiritual sons and daughters throughout the world. We Catholics are one body, one body in Christ, and whoever strikes unjustly at one of us strikes at all.

The Communist understands this. He well knows that in striking at the hierarchy, while professing to spare or even to sustain the laity, he is making his most effective blow at Catholicism—and he knows that in striking at Catholicism, he is delivering his most effective blow at organized religion of every kind. Why else would a Catholic prelate, like Archbishop Paul Yu Pin, be assailed so often by the Communists in dismembered China? The Catholics are a negligible percentage of the population of China, probably two per cent. Catholic representation in the political life of China does not amount to a row of beans. Catholic holdings in the economic life of China would have no significance whatsoever. Even in the limited area of such finances or properties as may belong to missionary groups in China, Catholic holdings would prove very much less than those of the prosperous Protestant missionary foundations. But when the Communist radio announced in China those whom the party would strike, it was a Catholic archbishop who was named first. Catholic priests and religious have the sublime privilege of being selected for special persecution, though their Protestant brothers have suffered as well.

Why? For the exact same reason that the Holy Father and the Catholic hierarchy are made the constant object of communist abuse and fellow-traveler criticism in every corner of the world. How many of you can name any of the dozens of Protestant diplomats or agnostic university presidents or creedless authors or other American, English, and European non-Catholic personalities who at one time or another in the long history of Italian Fascism spoke warm words of admiration for this, that or the other aspect of Mussolini's administration? And yet day in, day out, the world is reminded by the red fascists and by fellow-travelers of every fugitive phrase uttered by a Catholic prelate, whatever the circumstances or whatever the context, with regard to the government which existed in Italy for two solid decades, with regard to Ethiopia or any aspect of the struggles there, with regard to Spain and the tremendously complex upheaval there or with regard to any other issue of a mixed kind where any possible case, however specious, can be made against a member of the Catholic hierarchy. Not occasionally, mind you, but day in, day out—all in the effort to achieve a frankly avowed communist aim: the isolation of the Holy See from the Catholic community dispersed throughout the world.

That is the first lesson to be learned about communist tactics; it is the first objective in communist strategy with regard to religion. All else takes on its meaning from that central purpose; the breaking of diplomatic relations with the Vatican by nations which traditionally carried on those relations in their own interest and at their own wish; the suppression of the Catholic press and the interference with free correspondence between the faithful and the hierarchy within a nation and between the hierarchy and the Holy See in the international community; the whispering campaigns in Italy; the beatings of the bishops in Trieste; the dumb-show of the trials in Yugoslavia and in Hungary; the defamations in Poland and Czechoslovakia; the enforced "reversions" of the Catholic Eastern churches in the Ukraine and Rumania. It is only in the total pattern with these that the Hungarian Cardinal's fate may be understood.

What lessons should you and I, Catholics here in America, derive from all this? Well, the first and most obvious lesson is that as Catholics we must recognize anew what we should never have forgotten for a single moment: our spiritual solidarity with all those who believe in Christ and who love His Church on whatever level and in whatever land, wherever in the world Catholics are to be found. We must recognize with our intellects and embrace with our wills all the great dogmas of the unity and universality of the visible Church. We must meditate constantly and apply practically the social and even political implications of the doctrine of the Mystical Body of Christ, the dogma of the communion of saints, the fact that Catholicism brings together in a single family, at once human and divine, all those anywhere who receive its sacraments. Against the pretensions of world communism we must reaffirm the principles of world "communionism," to use the happy phrase by which one of our number has designated Catholicism. We must talk much less in terms which imply any species of division among us, even legitimate division, and we must emphasize at all times the elements of our essential unity. We must not talk of Eastern Catholics or Western Catholics, or Irish Catholics or German Catholics or French Catholics or Italian Catholics or American Catholics or Chinese Catholics. We must talk of Catholics—and we must know and pray and bother about Catholics in Ireland and Germany and France and Italy and China and Poland and Lithuania and Hungary and Africa and Australia and Russia and India and South America and elsewhere from the largest continent like Asia to the smallest islands like Malta. That is the first point: the need of reawakening our world-consciousness as Catholics, the members of Christ's International, the International that abides, even as Christ abides, yesterday, today and forever the same. In this way we shall prevent by anticipation the communist tactic of operating on a world level against us on a local basis: the tactic of using world radio, world press, world congresses and other world channels to defame us in Spain while professing to admire us elsewhere; or to discredit us in Yugoslavia while professing to dissociate our brethren there from us here. Thus, too, we shall build in ever greater beauty of unity and strength the world ramparts of the city of God on earth which is the Church, against which world communism principally conspires and upon which world peace principally depends.

In this connection, I should like to say something here tonight that I am confident Cardinal Mindszenty would say if he could stand before you for one free minute and speak his mind without fear of physical and moral consequences to his nation and his flock. These, of course, are the principal poisons and means of blackmail used against him and against every bishop by the red fascists. The Cardinal would thank you for every protest you voice and every action you take against the indignities which have been heaped upon his individual person. But he would remind you, I feel confident, that just as the indignities done him as a Cardinal make him a symbol of the red fascist attack on religion, so the indignities done him as a man make him a symbol of the millions who suffer under red fascism. The Cardinal's conviction and life sentence for doing his simple duty as a free citizen and as a Cardinal, while highly dramatic because of his position as Primate of Hungary, should not be considered isolated offences on the part of the red fascists. The Cardinal would say to you, as would any worthy priest, that while his privileges as a prelate have been outraged, his essential rights as a man have no less certainly been done violence—and in this latter respect he shares the fate of millions overwhelmed by the waves of oppression which have been sweeping over the Russian border into European countries for these several years. The Cardinal would ask you to pray for him, to be sure, and to work for his release—but he would ask you no less certainly to remember with prayers and protests the fathers of families, the valiant sons, the humble workers, the conscientious professional men, the thousands of teachers and tradesmen and simple citizens who are imprisoned within the boundaries of their once free nations. Despite his position as a Cardinal, indeed because of his position, the Cardinal's sense of Catholic solidarity with all who suffer would prompt him to remind you tonight of the fate of his fellow-prisoners and of their families throughout Eastern Europe—and to beg your prayers for them. As Catholics, the lesson we must carry out of the present crisis is that of the necessity of prayer, of solidarity in prayer, of the efficacy of prayer.

Secondly, as Americans we must recognize the necessity for a return to the first principles, moral and political, upon which the religious and civil liberties of this land repose. We must reaffirm these principles in lively fashion. We must not take them for granted, for liberty taken for granted, like love taken for granted, speedily dies. We must see to it that our children are reared in the tradition by which our fathers were made free men—proud, prosperous, independent and pious. We must recognize that those principles are under attack here at home quite as much as they are abroad, even though the war against them be further advanced in Eastern Europe than it is in Western Europe and in Western Europe than it is here at home.

We would do well to recall that most ideas, good and bad, originate like the sun in the East. Like the sun, they are always later in arriving in our longitudes than they are in spreading over Europe. It might be well to remember the hour differences in the mere measurement of time as between Moscow and Berlin and London and New York and Chicago and the West Coast. Here in Chicago you are a couple of hours behind New York in the mere advent of the sun out of the east. New York is about six hours behind Europe, Europe a few hours behind the East. So ideas, policies, schemes can likewise advance bit by bit out of the East.

The great difference is this: the sun and the measurements of time move on the fatal level of the physical. The spread of ideas and, more particularly, the adoption of programs and schemes are on the level of the human, the moral and therefore the free. Their progress is not fatal. It can be stopped. Some ideas can be resisted and overcome by better ideas. Some programs can be prevented in their progress by the establishment of better programs. When you read what is happening in Eastern Europe and what threatens to happen in Central Europe, be mindful of the time-schedule by which the sun moves fatally westward. But do not make the mistake of supposing that evil ideas need travel with equal fatality. It can happen here—but it need not. Oriental despotism can move into our national life only if we leave the way open for it to do so. Accordingly, we must develop our every reserve of national, moral and political idealism. We must study the origin and the rise of American institutions and we must teach their story to our children. We must refresh our memories concerning the reasons which brought our ancestors to these shores and we must recapture their determination that those reasons never be present in the American nation. We must deal with American justice, but with American realism, with those who would subvert our institutions or destroy our traditions. We must not allow any specious plea of civil liberties to warrant a license to our would-be assassins. We must not permit a tolerance of persons to become a tolerance of errors, particularly of dynamic errors which carry with them the seeds of our national destruction.

Thirdly, both as Catholics and as Americans, on grounds both supernatural and natural, we must devise some means of turning the age of the fish into an age of humanity—of bringing back into the eye of the fish the life, the light and the love of a man, a child of God. We shall do that, of course, by faith, by hope, by charity, by all the Christian virtues which the Church exists to preach and the Knights of Columbus exist to spread. But in order effectively to put the forces of Christian virtue in the field, we must have a precise enemy against which to drive them. That enemy here in America, that most important enemy, the enemy who turns men's hearts and eyes into those of the age of the fish and therefore leaves men susceptible to the snares of communism, is cynicism. We must at all costs escape the danger of cynicism. We must not permit the headlines of the day, or even the worst things that have happened at home or abroad, so to fray our nerves or to disturb our hearts or to upset our spleens as to make us forget the calm, the dignity, the poise of spirit and the stability of mind which Christ requires of His disciples no matter what befall them. When the tempest rages and we, like Peter of old, are prompted to protest against our testing, we must remind ourselves of the voice of Christ: "Why are ye afraid, O ye of little faith?" Under no circumstances may we permit the picture in the papers, or the things we are hearing by radio to make us lose the vision which should be ours as Catholic Christians, or otherwise to fall victim to that cynicism which underlies the age of the fish.

Our prayers go out to all abroad, to those whom our deeds cannot reach. Our patient work must be done here at home, in the land where God placed us. Those prayers and that patience will be rightly rewarded. Just as surely as tonight the Iron Curtain has fallen around Christian peoples, so one day it will part again as the mist before the springtime sun. Let no one be discouraged. God is not mocked and

His will is not forever frustrated. Our prayers will be answered and the Iron Curtain will rise. Our work at home will bear fruit and when the Iron Curtain rises the devout peoples who will then rejoin us in the free assemblies of the world will find intact in America the Christian values and democratic institutions which now become ours for the safekeeping. I know not when the day of delivery will come—but when it does, may the people of Poland and Yugoslavia and Lithuania and Hungary find us more united than ever, more devout than before, more militantly for God, more ready to help all His children find their way back to Him in faith and freedom.

Communism's Deceptive Kindness †

Last week our Holy Father the Pope spoke of an enemy, worldwide in his activity and his evil aspirations, who is determined to rid the world of Catholicism, of Christ, and finally God. The Holy Father did not name the enemy; there was no need that he do so. Any child now knows the name of the organized foe of Christian civilization. Not every child, but only the child of God, knows the hard core of communist doctrine and therefore understands why the Franciscan message to the world is so urgently needed to defeat this enemy in our day.

The hard core of communism is materialism. The heart of the Franciscan message is the reality, the primacy and the beauty of the spiritual. There in two sentences you have the secret of communist brutality and the secret of Christian patience. Of one the master is Marx; of the other the patron is St. Francis.

The enemy which confronts us on every side today is materialism. True, there are varying degrees of intensity in his attack, but everywhere his basic characteristic is godlessness.

Materialism reveals itself in its most violent, ruth-

† Address delivered at the national convention of the Third Order of St. Francis at Milwaukee, October, 1952.

less forms in those countries which are dominated by communism. Communism is so blatantly materialist that many people, appalled by its extremes, instinctively oppose it, but they do so without seriously disagreeing with it. Their opposition is to its murders, not to its materialism.

Accordingly, their opposition is really on shaky foundations and might easily turn to support if communism ever became more polite. Such people find communism unpleasant, but not false. They dislike it because it resorts to brutality, not because it is based on evil ideas. They denounce it, not because it is contrary to the nature of things but because it is cruel.

They thus lay themselves open to the suspicion that they would accept it if it were kind. That is precisely what many people are prepared to do; they are content to rest their objection to communism on the mere fact that it is unkind. They do not see how appalling is its complete materialism because they themselves are materialists; they are kind materialists, gentle materialists, refined materialists—but they are materialists all the same.

If they were not, they would themselves perceive that the cruelty of communism springs from its denial of human dignity, while this in turn springs from the denial of God. With a very little reflection, they would understand that communism's denial of God is the consequence of its materialism—and that they are themselves infected with the virus which eventually brutalizes all materialistic systems, even as it has done to communism.

We cannot conquer the materialism of communism with any system of thought which is equally materialist but merely more kind. The materialist's answer to communism is futile and those who are themselves communist will never even understand, let alone remove, the evil of organized atheism.

Fortunately, we cannot say that communism has gained the day in our country, but we assuredly cannot be optimistic about materialism. The fact is that wherever God is discarded and the spiritual purpose of life is obscured, men speedily conceive their destinies in strictly earthly terms and therefore within a strictly materialist pattern. Their standard of values becomes one of achievement measurable in material terms rather than one of spiritual growth expressed in moral terms. This is materialism pure and simple. It differs from communism in degree, not in kind.

Such materialism goes by different names. Sometimes the names, like the people who wear them, are kindly; such names are humanitarianism and philanthropy. Sometimes the name is political and the people to whom it applies are engaged in political action; such a name is socialism. Sometimes the name is an evasive term which seeks to avoid the stigmas attached to more exact names; so we have talk about "welfare states" to avoid talking about socialism.

But underneath all these names lies a basic materialism which is of their essence. All these systems, when they use Christian vocabulary, identify the Christian way of life with material benefit, not with spiritual growth. They find the end and purpose of man in social accomplishments here below, not in eternal salvation hereafter. They have kindly, generous, even self-sacrificing exponents in the case of many of them. But the welfare they promote, like the vision which inspires them, is strictly material; it is earthbound and therefore godless.

Some of them, indeed many, are passionately opposed to despotism. Their opposition, however, is pathetic—since the philosophies they preach have in them the fatal seeds of totalitarianism. All materialism is fatally totalitarian. Whatever excludes God and the spiritual, limits values not merely to the things of this world but also to the powers of this world.

The supreme power of this world is always Caesar, and when he has neither rival, nor challenge, nor control, nor superior, he is a tyrant in the strict sense of the word. Sometimes he is a pleasant tyrant; sometimes he is a paternal tyrant; sometimes he is even a gentle tyrant. But these are questions of personality, not of principle: in principle, powers which do not include homage to God and deference to the spiritual are despotic.

To what extent God is left out of our contemporary life, it is difficult to say. This much is certain. Not all those who talk of God believe in Him, and many use the word "spiritual" who would have no part of the reality. Paganism is much more entrenched than we would care to admit. Christians stand in danger of failing to appreciate how dangerous is the consequent situation. Sometimes you hear devout people say: "Most of the pagans I know keep their ideas to themselves. Their paganism is purely a private thing.

They are not missionaries of materialism. They don't try to convert people to it. They leave the rest of us free to be as spiritual-minded as we choose."

All this may be true; but the danger is that the pagans in our society by the very dead weight of their numbers may completely crush the influence of all others; so that all may succumb to the dead pressure of materialism.

However, this is not a true picture of the pagan attitude. That attitude is really aggressive and so the Christian is not free to remain impassive, inactive, inoperative in society. Christ described the Christian's function within the world in terms of yeast; the pagan majority may be inert and materialist, but the believing element of society, whether lesser or greater in number, is called upon actively to change the tone of the world: to be apostles, evangelists, teachers by word and example, heralds of the Great King.

This is the Franciscan message to our generation: that we may not keep the kingdom of God to ourselves, but must spread it or it will die within us.

Clearly the impact of any one of us on the materialist mass around him will vary according to his own conviction, courage and holy zeal as well as according to the receptivity of the pagan world nearest to him. The variations in effectiveness are questions of degree; the essential thing is that each Christian be an apostle, or, in the phrase of St. Francis, a herald of Christ's gospel. *"Praeco sum magni regis."* So cried Francis: "I am the herald of the Great King." So must cry each of us.

We have said that each Christian must do his part as a herald of the Great King, that all are called to help change the tone of society from one of materialism to one of spirituality. But over and above this constant work of the believing multitude, there is required the activity of leaders. The conflict is between the masses of pagan materialism and the multitudes of Christian believers. But there is also a conflict between the leaders of these two camps. That is why we must watch at all times for opportunities to replace materialistic leadership with spiritual leadership at every post where rival leaders are contending to grasp authority.

I say this in no partisan sense whatever and my intent is quite the reverse of political. But each should weigh the principle in his own political decisions; we should be constantly on the lookout, locally, nationally and internationally, for men and women who crown their political or professional abilities with spiritual vision and devotion to spiritual values. It is not playing politics to say that one of the tests of political leadership should be the spiritual insight of the would-be statesman; we badly need political leaders with spiritual vision. We always need them.

Similarly, we need spiritual vision in our teachers, doctors, writers, lawyers, trade unionists, workers and managers. Every level of society is riddled with materialism; every level must be transformed by spirituality. That is the Franciscan message to our generation.

Sometimes people ask questions like: "What field

would St. Francis choose as the principal channel of his apostolate in our day?" I think I know the answer to that question; it is suggested by the example he gave in his own day. St. Francis used all the channels of communication which were open to his generation: he preached to the people, he composed the verses of his poetry, he sang the songs of the troubadours. This means to me that if he were alive today he would use the press, radio, television, movies, and all channels which provoke, promote or perfect the thought of the people, the exercise of their minds.

The appeal of St. Francis might be superficially to the senses and the emotions, but it would be ultimately to the thinking and to the intellect of our generation.

It is precisely on this level, the level of thought and intellect, that the chief battle between materialism and Christianity is being waged in our day.

More and more these days people are motivated primarily by a degrading mixture of sensuality, sensationalism, political prejudice and selfish opportunism. So the way is paved, gradually but inevitably, for the managers who will hold the ring and provide the bread and circuses and security which are all the modern "masses" appear to require. This is and must be the trend in a country as deeply materialist as ours.

One is not asking that we become intellectuals, for most of us are incapable of that, but that, according to the measure of our capacity, we be intellectual, use our intellect and will in our lives, behave, that is, like human beings. How else can the present trend toward inhumanity be countered except by people behaving like human beings? To the extent that such an effort is made by anyone, a point of resistance is set up to the materialism which is corroding our country and stripping it of its soul.

The communist is taught from the first to use his knowledge as a weapon. It is assumed that, just because he is a communist, he will have the zeal to acquire a working knowledge of his creed, to learn the technique necessary to impart it and to lose no opportunity of using both to further the evil cause for which his party stands. From his first moment of entry into its ranks he is trained to be an apostle and he is successful in his apostolate, not merely because of his own zeal, but because he is hardly anywhere sufficiently opposed by competent effort on our part that is equally well trained, courageous and personal.

Thus, in the middle and lower classes of American life, he and the materialists, who consciously or subconsciously support his ideals, hold the intellectual initiative. They will continue to do so until we train ourselves to go over to the attack.

You never have any trouble getting thousands to gather to hear you talk; believe me, I know. But with all our colleges and universities and study clubs, it is worth your life to get a half-dozen people who will stand up and be heard—and worth your life twice to get half that number who will be worth hearing. The fact is millions love the faith enough to die for it; few have studied it hard enough to be able to defend it. If St. Francis were here today he would establish a school for preachers and lay speakers on the faith.

So many think that they can be given painlessly and in tabloid form a collection of clichés that will turn them overnight into defenders of their faith. They should disillusion themselves with the steady realization that they can get nothing without sweat. Until more are prepared for this grind that is required of them, claims that "the laity would like to play a part in the apostolate" will ring somewhat hollow. The lead has been given but the follow-up has not been conspicuous. This is because the follow-up requires effort; and that is just what so many of us are not quite prepared to give.

From what has just been said, I would except the faithful few, the gloriously inconspicuous few who are speaking up for the spiritual with tireless courage. I would salute them here for what they are—the salt of the earth, the light of the world, the champions of all we hold dear. The Third Order members are samples. My whole plea is that their number should be increased. Until it is, the fight will go against us—and St. Francis will be overrun by Marx. I don't think he can be!